From Main Street to Wall Street

A Beginner's Guide to Success on The Street

Alex Gennaro

With Gary Kelman

Copyright © 2018 Alex Gennaro

Hardcover ISBN: 978-1-63263-757-4
Paperback ISBN: 978-1-63263-758-1

All rights reserved. No part of this publication may be reproduced, stored in a retrieval system, or transmitted in any form or by any means, electronic, mechanical, recording or otherwise, without the prior written permission of the author.

Published by BookLocker.com, Inc., St. Petersburg, Florida.

Printed on acid-free paper.

BookLocker.com, Inc.
2018

First Edition

DEDICATION

To my parents, my mentors, and all who stood behind me, and beside me, through thick and thin, and all that's in between…

And a special tip of the cap to my co-author Gary Kelman, whose guidance and encouragement helped make my vision a reality

DISCLAIMER

This book details the author's personal experiences with and opinions about securing a job on Wall Street. The author is not writing or representing himself as a licensed representative of any firm or institution.

The author and publisher are providing this book and its contents on an "as is" basis and make no representations or warranties of any kind with respect to this book or its contents. The author and publisher disclaim all such representations and warranties, including for example warranties of merchantability and any advice for a particular purpose. In addition, the author and publisher do not represent or warrant that the information accessible via this book is accurate, complete, or current.

The statements made about products and services have not been evaluated by the U.S. government. Please consult with your own legal, accounting, financial, or other licensed professional regarding the suggestions and recommendations made in this book.

Except as specifically stated in this book, neither the author or publisher, nor any authors, contributors, or other representatives will be liable for damages arising out of or in connection with the use of this book. This is a comprehensive limitation of liability that applies to all damages of any kind, including (without limitation) compensatory; direct, indirect, or consequential damages; loss of data, income, or profit; loss of or damage to property and claims of third parties.

From Main Street to Wall Street

You understand that this book is not intended as a substitute for consultation with a licensed legal, financial, or accounting professional. Before you change your lifestyle in any way, you are advised to consult a licensed professional to ensure that you are doing what's best for your situation.

This book provides content related to Wall Street and related topics. As such, use of this book implies your acceptance of this disclaimer.

TABLE OF CONTENTS

Introduction/Prologue 1

CHAPTER ONE: MY (BACK) STORY 3

    Growing Up 3
    My Undergraduate Career..5
    The Lean Years 5
    The Turning Point 6
    Semester Abroad..7
    Born Again 8
    Finding (and following) My Path....................................9

CHAPTER TWO: MY TAKEAWAYS FROM COLLEGE......**11**

    Setting Yourself Up For Success 11
    Alternative Pathways 12
    Early Networking...13
    Extracurricular Activities / Clubs 13
    Career Fairs..14

CHAPTER THREE: PREPARATORY SKILLS/ CERTIFICATIONS
    TO MAKE YOU MORE MARKETABLE (JOB WORTHY) **17**

    Creating Your CV 19
    Series Tests 21

CHAPTER FOUR: NETWORKING....................................**25**

CHAPTER FIVE: CREATE YOUR
    OWN OPPORTUNITIES **27**

CHAPTER SIX: INTERVIEWING **33**

    Social Media 33
    The Interview Proper (or the Proper Interview)............34
    Screening..36

CHAPTER SEVEN: ON THE JOB!! **39**

    Where To Live? 39
    Dressing At Work 40

From Main Street to Wall Street

Personal Styling 43
Eating Lunch at Work 44

CHAPTER EIGHT: COMPLETING YOUR WORK **47**

CYA 48

CHAPTER NINE: COMPANY SOCIALS **51**

Office Relationships 52

CHAPTER TEN: BE PROACTIVE **55**

**CHAPTER ELEVEN: GENERAL TIPS FOR
SUCCESS AT WORK** **57**

Tools 57
Meetings 59
Corresponding with Your Superiors 61
Smart Phones 61
Desk Top 62
(Almost) Always Volunteer 63
Connecting with your Manager 63
Give Everyone Respect 65
Naming Files 65
Front/Middle/Back Office 66
Work Hours 67
Outside Business Interests 68
SWOT 69

**CHAPTER TWELVE: COMMUNICATION
USING FIRM EQUIPMENT** **71**

CHAPTER THIRTEEN: ALWAYS BE PREPARED **73**

The View From The Bottom 74

CHAPTER FOURTEEN: VACATION **75**

**CHAPTER FIFTEEN: COMPANY CREDIT CARD /
WORKING LATE** **79**

**CHAPTER SIXTEEN: WHAT TO DO WHEN TIMES ARE
ROUGH AND THINGS AREN'T GOING AS WELL
AS YOU HOPED** **81**

viii

A Beginner's Guide to Success On The Street

My Personal Trials, Challenges, and Road Map to the
Promised Land 81

CHAPTER SEVENTEEN: PERSONAL GROWTH **89**

Investing / Retirement Savings 89

The Ten Commandments **91**

Epilogue **93**

Glossary **95**

Introduction/Prologue

The road to the Promised Land is never an easy one. For those who aren't mavericks or wonder boys, the amount of effort required to get yourself on "The Street" is immense and intense. There is usually one of four scenarios in which one finds him/herself on Wall Street:

- There is the one who knew from a young age he wanted to work there. His Dad or neighbors worked in Finance, and he was always very savvy, possibly entrepreneurial, and good with managing money.
- The second is someone who discovers he/she likes Finance in college. He went in not knowing what he wanted to do with his life. Then he took a Finance/Accounting class, an Economics class, or even a Statistics class and had an "ah hah" moment when he realized that this is for him.
- Another demographic is that large club of people who simply want to make a lot of money, be rich, live that lifestyle—and they think that The Street is paved with gold.
- Finally, which is the rarest, is the young established professional who makes a career change because he is unhappy or bored with his current profession; usually disillusioned lawyers or doctors, but occasionally other professionals as well.

This book is intended to help position you successfully as a young college student or graduate for a job on Wall Street, and then, once there, to help you keep it.

CHAPTER ONE: MY (BACK) STORY

Growing Up

I was scenarios one and three (see above). Before I even knew what the concept of money was, my favorite color was green. Maybe that happened to be a coincidence, but I think not. It was more kismet, karma, call it what you will; but fate had a hand. As I grew older I began to grow more interested in money: the smell of a freshly minted dollar bill, the crisp rigidity of one that you know had been printed recently was a great feeling to me! I also began collecting different currencies, and still do to this day. It began when I was around five or so and my uncle gave me a silver dollar and half dollar. That sparked my interest immediately, and, from then on, every time I visited my extended family, he would give me a new coin or bill that usually became more exotic as I got older. To this day I collect currencies as I travel around the world and keep a big bag of mixed currency in a safety deposit box. It's a representation of my interest not only in money in general, but of the places I've traveled to in the world as well as my interest in history and the history of money/currency in different cultures.

My parents were (and still are) both successful surgeons. However, like many doctors, money was a byproduct to them. Their focus and their lives were devoted and dedicated to taking care of their patients, no matter what the personal cost and sacrifice, no matter what the "return on their investment." Of course they liked to enjoy nice vacations, and had good taste in food and wine and restaurants. Who doesn't? But the making and investing of money was never truly of interest to them. They never focused on their own investments, and didn't pay very much attention to financial markets (only occasionally to see how their IRAs and 401Ks were doing). They generated enough income to cover their overhead (personal and professional), and that was enough and all that mattered to them. They had neither the time nor the inclination to watch every dollar, coming in or going out. Situations in which they could reduce personal or business expenses were not of general concern to them and often a bother. There was simply too little time for that. Whereas to me it always seemed natural that you should do whatever possible to grow your bottom line, whether by increasing your income or reducing your overhead. By minimizing your costs, at the end of the day, you take home more money. It's as simple and, to me, as intuitive as that.

I always liked Medicine, and briefly thought about becoming a doctor. I worked during two summers of high school as an orderly/transporter in the operating room of our local hospital, which was nice because I became friends with the nurses, physicians, and staff there, and part of the medical community to which my parents belonged. I also got to see my parents every day, which was really a plus considering I didn't see them as much during the year when I was at school and then at sports practices, and they were working late at the office or in surgery.

My interest in Finance and particularly Wall Street and the stock market has come in waves. I was first truly and profoundly introduced to the concept by my current Financial Advisor. He had adopted two sons from Russia, one of whom was my age. I met him initially when he brought his son to class to introduce him to everyone. And I became friendly with his son despite the language barrier; in fact, he spoke *zero English* at the time. Through that connection I grew to know his parents well. Later on in the year, he brought his Dad to school in a "bring your parent to class" day in which he explained what he did as a Financial Advisor, buying and selling stocks for clients and advising them how to protect and grow their wealth. That first lesson briefly piqued my interest, which then returned to hibernation status as I continued my life as a 12 year old (6th grader).

I would subsequently regain interest in the mystery of Finance towards the end of high school as I was granted limited access to the portfolio account that my grandfather, of blessed memory, had set up for me. He was a CPA, and had amassed a respectable amount of money by investing in conservative blue chip stocks with large dividends and bonds. As I became more involved I connected with another classmate/friend who was savvier and more knowledgeable than I. His father was a trader on Wall Street and began teaching his son at an early age all about investing and trading. He would then pass on some of those pearls to me, which I happily absorbed. Coincidentally we now both work at the same Wall Street firm and continue to bounce ideas off each other regularly.

<u>My Undergraduate Career</u>

<u>The Lean Years</u>

When I began applying for colleges, I looked for schools I thought I would have fun at, but also that had good undergraduate business programs. I ended up at the Kelley School of Business at Indiana University. At the time it was ranked in the top 25 (but little did I know that by the time I would graduate it would be ranked in the top five!). Unfortunately I did not graduate with a Kelley degree (I graduated with a general BA from Indiana University, which, in and of itself, is still very respectable). When I got to college, I arrived with a poor work ethic, having studied minimally in high school, yet still graduated with mostly grades from B+ to a few As. But I was not in the elite of my high school class and so I had a lot to learn about studying habits. Going to college in general is a big shock from high school, but going to a school in the Big 10, with 45K undergraduate students, was like a mind explosion. My first semester I rushed a few fraternities, did not find one that I really liked, but went out often and somehow still managed to do ok. I believe I finished with a 3.0 that semester. Usually people that are going to do poorly in college start out with a bad first semester. My above average first semester gave me a false sense of confidence, security, hope, and expectation that I had adjusted well to college life; and the second semester I sought to replicate what I had done the first semester, although this time I began pledging a fraternity while taking a heavier, harder class load. **Big mistake!!** The results were disastrous, as pledging takes up an enormous amount of your spare time. Those that were studious in high school were naturally equipped to budget their free time between studying for exams and pledging the frat. Those who were not (like me) had an extremely hard time managing pledging, studying, and trying to fit in fun time to relax. I finished the semester with around a 2.6 and was put on academic probation from Kelley.

<u>The Turning Point</u>

After pledging the fraternity, I had more free time to get back on track and the beginning of my sophomore year I committed to getting off probation, which I did, and felt good about that. But as I began taking the harder business courses I did not put in the true work required and push myself to the absolute maximum (i.e. meeting with TAs, professors, getting tutors), and by the second semester of my sophomore year I was back to another sub-par performance. At that point I felt deflated and defeated, behind on credits, and hopeless that I could dig myself out. *The First Rule of Holes* is that when you're in one, you stop digging!! So to avoid falling even further, possibly hopelessly, behind, I switched out of the business school to a Political Science major. I enjoyed politics, and thought that if I committed to it, for the first time in my college career I could do well.

<u>Semester Abroad</u>

Studying abroad is a great idea. You become more cultured, it's an unbelievable experience, you meet great people from all across the world, and it's another talking point on interviews that will make you more interesting. Also if you study abroad in a country where you previously studied the language (high school, college), it gives you an opportunity to practice and become more fluent. In the global financial world, being bilingual can be a big plus and extra-added attraction to potential prospective employers. Of note is that in my freshman year I initially enrolled in Introductory Chinese classes with the expectation that the next great emerging market would be China, and fluency (or at least conversational familiarity) with Mandarin would be a big selling point for me when looking for jobs in Finance. Unfortunately a snafu in the Registrar's Office locked me out of more advanced courses in this discipline; so other than ordering Chinese food (*in Chinese)* from the local restaurant, that initiative didn't amount to much. I was very disappointed, and rightfully so. Knowing a second language can be very beneficial to your career in Finance (besides the fact that your manager, or, for an interview, the interviewer, will be impressed that you speak a second language). Some roles require fluency in another language, or list it on the application form as "strongly preferred". Even if your job does not require you to know another language, it does not mean that knowing it won't become important later on down the line, or help you procure an entry level position. If you grew up speaking another language (other than English) at home with your parents, list this as "native speaker" on your resume. If you studied a language in high school, you may want to try to continue with that language in college as it might be easier for you already having a background in it. For those looking to study a new language in college, I'd recommend trying to learn Mandarin, Cantonese, Japanese, Spanish, German (or English if it is not your first language). Knowledge of one of these "second languages" could be the critical skill set that separates you from the pack, enables you to move forward in your company over time, and could catapult you into becoming the Head of Europe, Latin America, Asia, or Asia ex-Japan.

<u>Born Again</u>

Even with my new (Political Science) major, I stayed interested and involved in Finance by participating in both the Undergraduate Investment Club and Private Wealth Management Club, where I engaged in mock investing competitions. I spent the following summer (entering my junior year) coming up with a strategy to (finally!) succeed. I took a manageable class load, dedicated myself to studying, getting up early before my classes started and going to the library, then going straight to the library after my classes were over, as well as getting up early on Saturday mornings before parties at the frat house, and Sunday mornings before I sat on the couch and watched football. *The plan worked.* I

A Beginner's Guide to Success On The Street

graduated one semester late due to my switch in majors and studying abroad, but every semester going forward I made the Executive Dean's List which meant achieving a 3.7 or above. **Lesson 1:** *Learn from my mistakes, so that you don't have to spend the rest of college digging yourself out of a hole. It ain't easy, and the upfront benefits of partying are outweighed by the back side costs of struggling to stay afloat...*

Finding (and following) My Path

As I moved through college I became more entrenched in, almost addicted to, what was going on in the financial markets. I started tuning in regularly to *Fast Money* and *Mad Money* with Jim Cramer, began reading the Wall Street Journal, and many other financial websites and publications including the financial blog *Seeking Alpha* (which I find to be very helpful even to this day). I grew more and more confident in my ability not only to synthesize financial market data, but also to create actionable ideas and investment theses, i.e. pick stocks I thought would do well. I had read articles by professional analysts and amateurs alike on *Seeking Alpha* and thought I could write one as well. So I did. Towards the end of college and right before I began my job I wrote over a dozen articles on different investment ideas. The thought process, research, writing, and feedback were all invaluable learning tools, even at that early stage of my career.

CHAPTER TWO: MY TAKEAWAYS FROM COLLEGE

Setting Yourself Up For Success

College is an unbelievable, unforgettable, irreplaceable, and unique time in life. You'll have some of your fondest memories there, and unfortunately it truly flies by. Most people honestly have no idea what they want to do when they arrive, but they do know one thing: *they want to have fun.* Uninhibited, unsupervised, unregulated, and uncensored fun is very new to most people in college. Many plan on joining fraternities and sororities to enrich their social lives, and I encourage them to do so. The one thing you have to be careful about is sinking your college career before it even gets off the ground. You obviously want to aim for the highest grades you can; but during your first semester, despite all the new stuff going on around you, you should still realistically aim to achieve no lower than a 3.0 average. The distractions, real and tempting as they are, be damned: if you goof off and get a very poor GPA your first semester, you will never dig yourself out of it (see *First Rule of Holes* above) even if you're scoring 4.0s every subsequent semester. Don't put yourself behind the eight ball; it's a bad place to be.

Pledging a fraternity, sorority, or just general partying and neglect of your studies is not a valid excuse or winning strategy, especially if your parents are paying for you.

When you go about selecting your courses for freshman year you don't want to be a hero, nor do you want to be a chump. As I said in the Prologue, most of us aren't superheroes, so bombarding yourself with 18 credits of hard courses, as admirable and attractive as that seems the summer before you start, is, in fact, asinine. On the flip side, taking 12 credits so you can relax for the first semester doesn't help get you adjusted to college (although if you are feeling nervous it would be better to take this option as you can always make up credits in the summer, and you should be able to get all A's with such a light load). Find the happy medium that suits and works for you. The ideal freshman semester should consist of 15/16 credits. One thing you should also be doing is making sure that all of your credits count towards *something*. Taking "rec" classes in your freshman year is probably not your best choice unless you are taking 15 credits and the rec class is a pass / fail course that has almost no work and doesn't take time away from your other more difficult and focused classes.

If you were a direct admit to the undergraduate business program, kudos to you! But if not, and you are looking to enter the business school of your university, it is important to take the necessary classes needed for entry, **and do well in them**. Backload other "general" requirements you may need to graduate, as your requirements will most likely change once you have entered the business school.

<u>Alternative Pathways</u>

A Business, Finance, Economics, or Accounting major used to be the traditional path to a job on Wall Street. With the world quickly becoming digitized the need for certain essential skills has increased. Becoming a Math, Computer Science, Informatics, or even Physics major will now help you stand apart from other applicants, and gain the competitive edge needed to succeed in the Finance world. Think out of the box, and separate yourself from the pack with marketable skills that make you special, unique, desirable, *and, hopefully, indispensable.*

FYI-- In 2018, JP Morgan's Asia-Pacific incoming analysts' class consisted of roughly 40% non-business majors (Engineering, Neuroscience, Psychology). A word to the wise is sufficient...

<u>Early Networking</u>

You should create a *LinkedIn* page when you get to college or at the end of your first year. The percentage of people using *LinkedIn* at an earlier age has skyrocketed since I've left college. Having a *LinkedIn* page young in life will allow people to keep an eye on you earlier in your career development. It also serves another important function: it will become your business contact book. Instead of having to save business cards or scribble down emails in a safe place, you can have everything stored in one digital location.

<u>Extracurricular Activities / Clubs</u>

When you were applying to colleges and universities, your guidance counselor probably explained to you that it was important to have charity work or interesting extracurricular activities to distinguish you from the other applicants. The same applies in college. Whether you're trying to get into an elite program within the business school, or applying for an internship or for a full time job, some of the extracurricular activities you did in college may be able to distinguish you, particularize you, and give you interesting things to talk about in an interview. There are plenty of Finance related clubs you can join such as an Undergraduate Investing

Club or Private Wealth Management Club. Often these are led by associate professors through whom you have access to tangible Wall Street products like a Bloomberg Terminal. These clubs will sometimes hold mock investing competitions where you and a team (or you solo) create a portfolio of securities that go head to head with each other. You manage that portfolio for the semester and the portfolio with the greatest returns wins. This is something you'll be able to speak about in depth in an interview: Why/how you chose these securities? What is your investing style and strategy? etc. In some rare cases, the school will choose a student to be on the Endowment Investment team. This is as close to "running money" in the real world as you'll get before you graduate (unless you invest in your personal account) and you should leap at the opportunity. There is usually a highly selective interview process, so **come prepared**. There are other competitions you can enter, mainly case studies on companies, which lend themselves more to a consulting role; but these can be very helpful as well.

Career Fairs

If you're a sophomore or junior, you'll be looking to attend career fairs. This is where (hopefully) the banks and financial services companies you're looking to join will show up, set up booths, and allow you to engage them. If you attend a "target school", then you will have the usual suspects show up. Otherwise, you're still not totally out of luck. You will probably have some smaller or regional firms show up, and, if they don't, you need to go to them, i.e. call/email them and apply online. The business firm's people attending these events are usually younger employees at the company, often alumni from your school sent there to take a look at the possible talent they can bring to the bank. It is

A Beginner's Guide to Success On The Street

a very informal process, although every student there will (should) be wearing a suit. **Come prepared** with a folder containing 20 copies of your resume; one can never be too prepared. You'll circle the fair and look for the firms you're most interested in and go chat with the person standing in front of the booth. Unless you have researched the company well, don't ask generalized questions. It is a waste of their time and yours. They will most likely ask you to walk them through your resume. Do so, but try to connect with them on a personal level. They will be scrutinizing your resume much more thoroughly after the fair, along with HR in the Home Office. You want to stand out, be memorable. They are less likely to remember that you have a 3.67 GPA as opposed to the fact that you have gone skydiving over 10 times around the world and climbed Mount Kilimanjaro. Ask for their business card, thank them, and then follow up the next day with an email saying it was very nice to meet them and that you'd love the opportunity to speak again.

If you are selected for a first round interview, it will most likely be over the phone unless you are near one of their major offices. If you crush that, you'll be selected for a "super day" which is a big deal. The call-back is key. This is usually when they fly you to New York and put you up in a hotel near their HQ. It will be a long day during which multiple people around the firm drill you with questions from early in the morning until the afternoon. If you impress them you will be offered an internship (or a real job if you are doing this senior year, but you really should try to have a job locked up by then). Now all you have to do is go kill your summer internship (if you're a junior) and hope that you get that return offer!

CHAPTER THREE: PREPARATORY SKILLS/ CERTIFICATIONS TO MAKE YOU MORE MARKETABLE (JOB WORTHY)

Skills are usually something you learn on the job. However there are a lot of things you can do in advance to prepare for life on Wall Street which will either help you hit the ground running, or make you a more interesting candidate when going in to interviews. Many, but not all, schools or business programs provide an introductory class to Microsoft Excel and/or Microsoft Access. Excel is probably the most important and applicable program that you will use while in Finance and, really, adult life in general. In these intro classes, and even 200 level classes, you will learn important skills such as creating formulae to add/subtract/multiply/divide large sums of numbers. You will also learn VBA macros, V-Lookups, index matching and pivot tables which are important for sorting through large data sets and building large models that you can use to plug and play going forward on the job. "Modeling", or creating forward looking/ predicting financial models, is an essential skill for those looking to go into investment banking, or equity research (and possibly Private Equity down the line; it's almost impossible to get in right away!)

[As an aside, PE is very prestigious, and the reason it's so hard to get into PE is because it is essentially "the buy side" of investment banking (I consider this really the sell side because you are working for companies instead of doing the stuff yourself.). The buy side of more markets-based roles would be hedge funds or asset management shops where the sell side would be as a sell side analyst or a sales trader. The real difference between the sell side and buy side is that when you're on the sell side you're almost always working for someone else, whereas on the buy side people are working for you; it is you and your investors' money, and you are actually making the investment decisions or buying the company. "Carried interest" is used in hedge funds as well, but is more prominent in Private Equity. It's essentially just a performance fee, but with special benefits (see below). If the person managing the fund has a greater return than they targeted, then they get a share of the profits in excess of their target. You are not eligible to participate in carried interest until you become much more senior at a fund. The reason why it is very "controversial" is because it is taxed as capital gains, not income, which ends up being a much better rate than if it were being taxed as a portion of salary. This is why a lot of partners at private equity shops or hedge funds elect to take, or set up, the fund this way with a large portion of their salary as carried interest.]

Descending from the giddy heights of PE to the peasant-style grinding of an entry level analyst, following orders and getting the job done, done right, and in a timely fashion is essential. Depending on your job, and your manager (boss), projects may be given with little notice, or you may be swamped with work already. Knowing key or command shortcuts are essential in Excel and can dramatically increase both the speed and efficiency at which you work in Excel. Some people even become proficient enough that they actually never use a mouse, and only use the keyboard functions (a very big plus; the sooner you master it, the better!).

Access is also important, but less vital. Microsoft Access is a program that allows you to essentially create databases of large sums of information that are sortable by extremely specific parameters. You will learn for both Access and Excel "what if" statements which allow you to create hypothetical scenarios to solve for or create a process for certain situations.

Lastly there is Microsoft PowerPoint/Word which most people know well from high school. I've never seen a course offered on how to really master these programs. But be sure you know how to put together a sophisticated PowerPoint presentation and a neat Word document. It is more important to have a "clean" looking presentation that is short and concise than a long drawn-out "artsy" looking one.

<u>Creating Your CV</u>

Writing a résumé or CV (curriculum vitae) is a skill. You could be a great candidate, but having an unorganized, unsophisticated looking CV shows you're either immature, don't care, or you're just plain sloppy and pay little attention to detail. None of the foregoing makes you an attractive candidate. **The devil is in the details** (a common theme I will repeat often in the coming chapters). It's the little things that count and can make all the difference. This may sound obvious and intuitive, but make sure that there are no misspelled words or grammatical errors. You'd be surprised but many resumes contain spelling errors which are looked at unfavorably and usually then tossed aside or put to the bottom of the stack. Consult with a professor, an established professional, or an online business template to make sure your resume looks professional. Your resume should not be longer than a page; you're a college student and can't possibly have the skills or experience to fill out multiple pages.

Don't overcook it! Not only that, but the interviewers don't have time to wade through a voluminous CV, likely filled with fluff (such as your high school clubs). No one cares about that and will likely lose interest before getting to the end anyway. Make it short, sweet, and to the point; emphasize your true accomplishments, or else the really good stuff you have to offer a prospective employer will be lost in the unimportant weeds. You won't fool anyone, especially HR at an established Finance firm, by including unnecessary extraneous information to polish your halo in an attempt to make you look better than you really are. Just include the relevant facts that will pique the interest of the reviewer. **Less is more**; be brief and to the point.

To make it stand out, the one thing I learned from taking a one credit resume building class in college is that you should always start the description of prior employment with a *verb*, i.e. "analyzed," "gathered," "synthesized." This helps portray a stronger *sense of action* in work. Also, no statements beginning with "I" (humility is a plus). "Buzzwords" are, for better or for worse, more important than you can imagine. A buzzword is a word or phrase that has meaning, importance, and fashionability at a particular time and in a particular context. Applications today are frequently scanned and pre-screened by computer programs that look for very specific buzzwords. If those words are present, the application (and candidate) is moved to the top of the heap; if not, they are deleted or stored for another time (not where you want to be). Check websites to see what a company is looking for. Certain buzzwords will crop up over and over; be certain those same words are in your CV, over and over and over again. It makes little sense to you and me, but the processing computer has a mind and marching orders of its own and will choose those candidates who know how to game the system. Be that person.

Series Tests

In the past, almost all certifications that you needed to interact with securities required sponsorship from your FINRA (Financial Industry Regulatory Authority) registered firm. This basically means that they vouch for you, and offer to pay your testing fees, exam, prep material fees, and sometimes even tutor fees.

Originally there were some, however, that did not require the backing of a firm. These are:

Series 3, 30, 31

Acquiring one of these licenses (depending on which area of Finance you're looking to step into) while in college should impress interviewers that you are extremely interested in the field and a serious and motivated person.

However, beginning October 1, 2018, FINRA is releasing a new exam called The Securities Industry Essentials (SIE, or Essentials) Exam. You do not need to be sponsored by a FINRA registered firm and you can take the exam as early as 18 years old.

According to FINRA's website, the exam "assesses a candidate's knowledge of basic securities industry information including concepts fundamental to working in the industry, such as types of products and their risks; the structure of the securities industry markets, regulatory agencies and their functions; and prohibited practices." It is supposed to consolidate a lot of the material present in many of the series exams today. The plan is for the SIE to incorporate a bulk of the material, and then, once you join a FINRA registered firm, the series exam(s) you need to take more specific to your job will be fewer and more focused. Due to the new regulations, those who are ambitious and interested in a career in

Finance should try to take this new test as early as possible, either in the summer before their freshman year of college, or in the summer after freshman year. Not only will it be very helpful for those applying for jobs on Wall Street after college, but it will probably help you get that summer internship the summer of your junior year that will help you land your fulltime gig. It is also important to note that these coveted internships are getting more and more competitive, and many kids in college are looking at getting summer internships at banks the summer after their *sophomore* year. The application window usually opens up in the early fall, and ends in the winter, specifically late December or early January. As soon as you return to college after the summer, you should begin monitoring these banks' career portals for internship applications, as you want to be one of the first to apply (*but definitely not to miss the deadline!*). The earlier you apply, the more time you have to try to lobby people at these banks, and use any political capital you have to get yourself into the most desirable internship programs.

The CFA

The Chartered Financial Analyst designation is extremely coveted, and difficult to obtain. It is one of the most challenging certifications to get as it is divided into three separate exams (Parts 1, 2, and 3). It is a **behemoth**, covering over ten topics including Accounting, Corporate Finance, Derivatives, Legislation and more. Most people taking the test are several years out of college, but there really is no reason a college upperclassman shouldn't be able to study and take the exam if he has a couple of Accounting and Corporate Finance classes under his belt. The earliest you can take the first leg of the CFA is your final year of college. **Having the first part of the CFA completed before you even begin**

A Beginner's Guide to Success On The Street

interviewing is profoundly more impressive than having a Series certification. The test takes an average of 250 hours of study before you should even feel comfortable taking the exam. But **it's worth its weight in gold if you can do it**. Looking back I wish I had applied myself more in this direction. It would have made my life so much easier going forward (see below).

An important caveat to note is that you don't receive the CFA distinction, even after you pass all three parts, until you have four years of work experience. So technically the earliest you can put the CFA letters after your name is age 25 as most people graduate college ~21 years old.

CHAPTER FOUR: NETWORKING

"If you're not networking, you're not working", a hackneyed cliché that is more profound and important than you realize. Networking is an important skill that should hopefully become more natural as you become older. You may not realize it but those teachers in high school, religious leaders, or family friends who wrote you letters of recommendation for college: that was a result of your networking with them. When you get to college you are going to meet professors, department chairs, guest lecturers, and recruiters that are all potential connections. When networking, it's important to not only get their business cards so you have their contact information, but also to **follow up promptly**. When you meet someone and then follow up months later (when you find him useful to you), he oftentimes may have forgotten who you are, or is less inclined to help because he sees through your transparency and that you are reaching out for a favor. An email the morning after you meet someone summarizing that it was nice to meet him, what your goals are, and that you look forward to staying in touch gives him a pleasant reminder of your encounter for down the road. **Mark my words—the devil is in the details**. This little seemingly insignificant detail may give you the best return on your investment. **It's not what you know, but who you know**. Right or wrong, truer words were never spoken.

You would be surprised, but people, even perfect strangers, *even superstars*, are often willing to speak/meet with you if you reach out.

From Main Street to Wall Street

In college I used to watch *Fast Money* and *Mad Money* pretty religiously. I liked many of the hosts of *Fast Money* and valued their opinions. I had already started working but was interested in a job on a trading desk as a sales trader. I thought I could kill two birds with one stone by asking to meet one of the hosts of the show and inquire about open positions. So I reached out to the head of Sales & Trading at Cowen. I physically mailed (USPS) some research articles I had recently written as well as sent them in an email to him. After I expressed my interest in the show, explaining that I was new to The Street, and had multiple career questions, he invited me to visit him on the set of *Fast Money*. It was a great experience. I showed up before the cameras started rolling and got to meet all of the traders. During the entire show I was standing right behind the video cameras. After the show concluded I was invited to grab dinner with them at Lavo, which started out as a nice get-together, and evolved into a rager by the end of the night. While no job came from the interaction, I gained another contact on Wall Street. **Big win!**

CHAPTER FIVE: CREATE YOUR OWN OPPORTUNITIES

As I've said, most opportunities in life don't fall into your lap. The best way to get a job on Wall Street is to get a meaningful and applicable undergraduate internship by doing well, and seeking help from professors in your undergraduate business program who usually have connections on Wall Street and can help set up interviews. At a sell side bulge bracket bank, at the bare minimum, usually 60% of interviewees get a return offer, and, on the greater end, 85% when the economy/Wall Street is doing well.

If you are not in an undergraduate Finance related major, the onus is on you to make things happen. Approach professors or heads of departments about seeking help with getting an internship or job. **Come prepared, and know your stuff.** They are not going to help a non-business school student if he isn't prepared and/or doesn't know generally what he wants.

Once you form a good relationship with this professor, ask if you can send him/her a *LinkedIn* invitation. Then ask if it is ok if you reach out to his connections. Oftentimes the people with whom Finance professors are connected (on *LinkedIn*) can become good connections and can be willing to help, depending on how good friends they are. If you get the ok, begin firing away on emails.

Don't reach out on *LinkedIn*. Most people don't check their *LinkedIn* page religiously whereas they do their work email. The general email address format for most firms on Wall Street is:

first.last@companyname.com

If you try an email in the above format and it doesn't go through, try their full name (so instead of "Alex" try "Alexander", Max/Maxwell etc). In some cases it's *first.middleinitial.last@companyname.com*

When you're emailing these individuals I recommend putting your "mutual connections name" in the subject field so they're more inclined to open an email from an outside email address.

In the email explain how you know your mutual connection, and then say you'd like to either meet him/her if possible or speak over the phone. Attach a resume. If you have applied to a job or internship, tell him that in the email. Don't simply ask for help—nobody wants to hear that from some random stranger, and likely won't respond in a positive way. Instead **ask if there is anything he thinks you can do to improve your chances**. This way it looks like you're hungry and willing to do whatever it takes to get ahead, rather than simply asking for a handout. A much better look.

If nothing concrete materializes after employing the strategies outlined above, it's time to take the next, slightly more aggressive, step. You have nothing to lose, if done properly, courteously, and inoffensively. After a general application online, you can look up people on *LinkedIn* who work in HR at the company. Email them (again try the formats I explained earlier) and say you really want the job and, **if there is anything you can do to improve your chances**, to please let you know. If you've reached a general HR switchboard, ask for the right person to contact, and follow-up with a similar call and conversation. Be prepared for plenty of frustration, disappointment, feelings of rejection, even despair! But keep your cool and stay the course. Dogged respectful persistence is the key to success here. Remember that in his day Babe

A Beginner's Guide to Success On The Street

Ruth was the greatest homerun hitter of all time. But he also had more strikeouts than anyone else. The lesson: it doesn't matter how many times you swing and miss; all you need is to connect and you're on your way to success.

The combined above methods is how I got my job on Wall Street. I called and emailed over a thousand people until I resonated with someone who had a mutual connection with me. I crushed my interviews and was eventually given a job. In a way I was like Bud Fox from *Wall Street*. The first time he meets Gordon Gekko, Gekko says "This is the kid, calls me 59 days in a row, wants to be a player. There ought to be a picture of you in the dictionary under persistence, kid." If you really want something, in this case a job working on Wall Street, you need to be extremely persistent to the point that you're almost hounding people. You may turn some people off, and others may continually tell you that they can't help you right now. **Or** they may be so tired of hearing from you that they find something in the firm just to get you off their back. Either way, that works! But continue to stay in touch with people and something may eventually open up. The connection which would eventually help me land my first job: **I called or emailed every two months for 15 months straight**. I never knew which, if any, connection(s) would be "the one", or if any job would materialize. But I kept the faith. Shoot a thousand arrows in the air and there's a good chance that one will hit the target. Fortunately, in my case, it did. Hopefully it will for you as well.

There are other ways to penetrate Wall Street. Look for "off cycle" internships on these companies' sites. They often list a winter internship. While not as prestigious as the summer internship, it may be easier to procure with fewer applicants in the winter months. It's still very valuable, and will get you that Wall Street "experience" for your resume.

If you've applied for desirable internships online without success, so what's next? It ain't over yet! Don't lose your mojo!! You can still make a positive impression and an impact—that's your endgame. **Do whatever it takes (*legitimately*) to make your resume stand out.** Besides e-mailing HR, you can try *physically* mailing a hard-copy of your resume and supporting documents (old school, but still worthwhile; you never know?). While that may seem excessive, **remember that you are competing with tens of thousands of other applicants, and you need to try to stand out in any way that you can.**

When I was on the hunt for my job, I was willing to take an off-cycle internship in the winter with the hope that it would evolve into a full time job if I worked my ass off. I had found an Investment Management internship that I really wanted in London, and wrote to several people there expressing why I wanted it, why I thought it would be a good fit, and that, even though I was older than the average person applying, they would not regret giving me the opportunity. When I didn't receive an email back, I decided to double down and stack the deck (what the hell? **Bury them in paper**). I printed out and (snail)mailed my resume and a few other documents to London (which wasn't cheap by the way), again expressing my interest in the Investment Management "programme" (as they say in the UK). Weeks later I received an email from HR in the Canary Wharf office saying that they had received my information and were very interested in speaking with me about joining the winter internship class. It just so happened that I received that email the day *after* I signed my full time job offer. While I was obviously more relieved to have a full time job, it was nice knowing that I had a backup plan if I didn't land the real deal, and that my continued persistence had been worth it. **Go the extra mile; it pays off.**

If you've mined all the above strategies and still nothing has popped, another thing you can try (although admittedly rarely successful) is reach out to banks, asset managers, and hedge funds, saying that you're hungry, will work long and hard hours, **and will work for free.** Somebody somewhere may have a need for free labor and will be impressed by your work ethic and dedication, and take you on. This approach wouldn't be my first choice, but it's an option, and if nothing else is working and you're desperate enough, I recommend it. Again, *when you have nothing, you have nothing to lose.* Follow the same format as before. Email whatever general email you can find for the company. The subject should read as "internship" or something along those lines. **Then attach 4 items. This is important:** A custom tailored cover letter, a resume, a list of contacts to whom they can reach out to verify your experience and character, and anything you may have worked on in Finance that demonstrates your skills.

The best sites I've come across for finding jobs in Finance are *Linkedin, efinancialcareers.com, onewire.com,* and *gobuyside.com.* I find that these are the sites that are providing actual jobs in Finance that people are looking for, and that people actively use the site and will reach out to you if they think you are a match. Do not waste your time with *Monster* or any of those general job websites; you won't find what you're looking for there.

CHAPTER SIX: INTERVIEWING

In Chapter Three I gave you skills on how to polish up your resume. Now I'll give you tips on how to do well in an interview.

But first:

Social Media

Almost everyone graduating college has some sort of social media account (likely multiple platforms), whether they be Facebook, Twitter, Instagram, or something else. Throughout college people often post inappropriate online data without thinking about the potential negative repercussions down the line. Recruiters in the twenty-first century have become tech savvy and now often screen applicants' social media profiles during the application process. Employers are looking to see what you do in your spare time, what type of life you live, and if you may be a liability to the firm? **The way to protect yourself is by making all your accounts private.** By doing so, no one can see your accounts without requesting access. The final thing left to do is make sure your profile picture on the account contains nothing taboo because that is the only thing they see when they find your account. Many people also use either a nickname or their first and middle name to make it more difficult to find. You could choose to make your account unsearchable, but that's very sketchy. The person vetting you might think that you have something to hide, which could be a huge red flag and put you at risk. We'd like to believe that our personal lives are personal, but they're really not, and you'd be surprised how transparent your inner self really is to those digging for information. **Sanitize your social media** unless you want to explain to an interviewer why you're smoking a bong in Punta Cana with your basket of deplorables.

The Interview Proper (or the Proper Interview)

Preparing for an interview will be different for every role and for every firm. If you are looking at a role in investment banking, you need to have your modeling skills down pat. For a role in asset management or on a trading desk, you should have a firm understanding of the financial markets, different types of investment products, general knowledge of the trading world, along with awareness of well-known asset managers and some brief familiarity with strategies. Sales & Trading interviews are usually broken down into three categories: Fit, Market, and Math/Brainteasers. The fit, or behavioral, questions are ones that you normally prepare for. Most of this section is explaining your resume, discussing your interest in the job, the firm, the industry, and things that may set you apart. A question often asked is "Why do you want to be a trader?" or "Why sales vs trading?" Market questions can range from stock pitches, to investing ideas, and how certain macro events affect certain markets. The last category is where people may struggle. The good news is that the math you'll be doing will really only be centered around *PEMDAS*, and, for those who don't remember from middle school, that's Parentheses, Exponents, Multiplication & Division, Addition & Subtraction. The bad news is that it will have to be mental math, so no calculators or writing it down on paper. If you're not good at mental math, try to use simple tricks; so, for example, if you can't do 13x13 quickly in your head, multiply 13x10 then 13x3 and add the two. The brainteasers can seem impossible, but it's less about getting them right and more about showing that you have a logical coherent thought process. However, if the brainteaser is a statistics question, they will look for accuracy. For private banking you should be cognizant of who your client base is, what kinds of services they want from the bank, and possibly how to cross-sell those items to the client. For more general Finance roles, just know the industry well along with any movements happening in the economy or political spectrum that could affect the firm.

You should know the names and backgrounds of the CEO and CFO of the firm, along with the person who heads the division you'll be joining. Overall understand what your firm is known for even if you're not joining the firm's bread and butter unit.

One thing people don't do enough of is stay current with the news. Before I landed my first job, several interviews I went on asked me what I thought about "XYZ" on the cover of the Wall Street Journal, or to tell them what I thought the most interesting article in the Financial Times was that morning and why. You should be able to tie in the subject to both Wall Street and domestic/international politics. Good financial sources you can use to stay current include the *Wall Street Journal*, *Financial Times*, *Bloomberg*, *Seeking Alpha*, *The Street*, *Investors Business Daily*, *Finviz*, *Motley Fool*, *Forbes*, *Yahoo Finance*, and *MarketWatch*. Oftentimes you will be told in advance who you are meeting with / being interviewed by. Prepare accordingly by looking them up on *LinkedIn* and becoming familiar with their past work history. If you can subtly insert that information into your interview they will most likely be impressed that you put in the time, effort, and initiative to know more about them in advance.

During the interview they may or may not ask you about what you do outside of the office. If given the opening, you should try to work this into the conversation, as well as your likes and dislikes. These extracurricular activities can make a big impact on whether you're hired. If it's between you and another candidate with a similar resume but you're more personable, relatable, and seem more fun, you're more likely to be hired. If you need further information on the types of questions you may get, salary information, or general questions in the industry, *Glassdoor*, *Wall Street Oasis*, and *Vault* are great resources.

<u>Screening</u>

Assuming you make it through all the interviews and receive a job offer (CONGRATULATIONS!!), the last stop before onboarding is screening (*deep vetting*). Firms will do comprehensive criminal background checks on you before you can start employment. Usually the bigger the firm, the more in-depth the checks are. **If you don't disclose that you've had an issue in the past and they find out, no matter how small it was, you're finished, done, kaput, screwed, in the weeds. Be honest**; for relatively minor things, such as a college drinking ticket, they may overlook it. **But dishonesty, failure to disclose, is the kiss of death. The cover-up is worse than the crime** (*see Richard Nixon*). Don't be an ass and think you're going to get away with something, because you won't. They're smarter than you and will find all the skeletons in your closet. Own your past. Lying and making false statements on your application is the unpardonable sin. Don't go there, no matter what. You'll never dig yourself out of that hole!

Now, having said that, assuming you've passed the background check, you may be asked to take a drug test. This is something you need

A Beginner's Guide to Success On The Street

to pass. If it's something you're nervous about, you should begin detoxing as soon as you begin interviewing, or even before if you want to be extra cautious. This is another potential minefield which will remain on your record **forever**. Don't be that guy who tests positive for marijuana. To you it's no big deal. On The Street, it's a big deal. You don't need that specter following and haunting you. Be smart, and **don't do dumb shit. It'll come back to bite you in the ass later on!** Enough said...

CHAPTER SEVEN: ON THE JOB!!

So you finally landed a job on The Street; now what?

Where To Live?

There's a lot to consider regarding your living situation once you receive a job offer. You may be itching to move into the city (NYC), but I'd caution you to be patient and lay out all your options. I recommend living at home for 2-4 months before you pull the trigger. It's important to build up a nest egg before you move in as Manhattan is expensive (more so than you think, with hidden costs everywhere). Having a few months' rent in your checking account will allow you to pay rent and enjoy life in the city without living paycheck to paycheck. I can't speak to other cities, but commuting into Manhattan from home, whether it be Long Island (LIRR), Westchester (Metro North), or New Jersey (Jersey Transit) is relatively simple. By delaying moving into the city, you can also look for an apartment in the winter which usually is easier to find and cheaper. Other major metropolitan areas are likely similar.

Once you have built up some cash reserves, it's time to look at apartments. Having a roommate vs living alone is a decision you'll have to make. The pros of having a roommate are that your rent will be significantly cheaper, and you have someone to hang out with after work. While it will be more expensive to live alone, if you prefer your peace and quiet, have tests to study for, or are single, this can be a better option. Most people look for a large true one bedroom, and then flex it (put up a fake wall). A two bedroom is preferable but way more expensive, and the one bedroom flex is a very workable compromise. The same goes for three people in a true two bedroom. The next thing you'll have to decide is *where* to live. I think it's better to live closer to work than choosing a cool area. I promise you, if you have the ability to walk to work, that's a luxury you'll never forget and never regret, and you'll never want to take the subway again. You can sleep later, and are not confined by the (un)reliability of the train schedule. You also won't have to pay for an unlimited subway (mass transit) pass every month, which is pricey (although if you're traveling through the city often it may just be worth it). The one thing I'll say is that if you decide to pick a place to live based on price, or because you believe a neighborhood fits your personality, make sure it is on the same side (East vs West) of Manhattan (or wherever you live and work) as your office. Taking multiple subways/buses on the way to work is not ideal (although if you're saving a lot of money rooming with someone, I get it).

<u>Dressing At Work</u>

The first thing you need to know is what to wear and how to show up on Monday morning of your first day. Sounds simple, no? Not so simple and intuitive as you might think. Every employer is different, every office is different, and every boss is different. In Finance, the rule of thumb has always been a suit to work. But times have changed, and Wall Street has seen many banks begin to OK "business casual". When you're first starting out, I highly recommend wearing a suit every day, or at the very least a pair of slacks, a sport jacket, and a tie. You may find that your boss not only encourages but prefers business casual. If this is the case you don't want to overshadow your boss, so wear business casual, and when there are big meetings you can break out the suit again. If your

A Beginner's Guide to Success On The Street

boss is not adamant about business casual, wear a suit. You can never go wrong with looking sharp. The one thing I absolutely hate though is slacks, a button down shirt, and a tie, no jacket. You look like a waiter when you do that. Obviously, if you are not wearing a jacket because you hung it up on your chair, that doesn't count.

There are three acceptable looks in Finance (and really life in general, in my humble opinion):

1. Full suit;
2. Suit no tie with one or two buttons from the shirt unbuttoned, handkerchief optional;
3. Business casual - no jacket, no tie, just slacks and a button down shirt.

Stick to these three looks, and I promise you won't look like a buffoon. The important thing to note if you're going "bizz caszh" is you should wear dark slacks. Khakis, chinos, or any derivative thereof is generally viewed as too casual for the office and, while people may not say anything, they will look down on it. More and more I've seen people wear more casual looking pants *a la* J Crew. While I think that's fine on occasion, I find it almost too casual a look. If you don't know what I'm talking about, think about the types of pants golfers wear. Regarding your shirt, you want it to be tight fitting; nothing is worse than a loose bunchy shirt. If you are slim, buy European cut shirts which will naturally be on the slimmer side. If you wear a regular fit that tends to be a little baggier, I have a suggestion for you. This technique works best if you wear boxer briefs instead of boxers because it will be tighter. In the morning, when you're getting dressed, tuck your shirt into your boxer briefs. The briefs should hug your waist tightly and then will draw in the shirt closer to your body. Make sure the boxers are not sticking out from

From Main Street to Wall Street

your slacks, though. The easiest way to do this is by putting on your button down shirt before your boxers, then slide the briefs up over the curt tails of your shirt and, once tucked in, push down an inch or so, so it's not peeking out of the top of your pants. Regardless of your approach to this technique, it should help make your shirt look like a fitted shirt.

I recently saw that they are making some sort of device to help with this, a jockstrap of sorts. It doesn't look too comfortable, so for now I'm sticking with my way.

In general, do not wear shirts with pockets or collar buttons. It's a very retro look and usually comes around as too casual. Once in a blue moon, on a Friday, is ok. A typical Finance look (especially trader) that ups the business casual look, which I call *business casual plus*, is rocking a company vest over the button down. It adds another layer to the outfit and allows you to rep your firm at the same time. Wearing a tie with business casual plus is ok. I don't know why, but if you wear the tie with this outfit and zip the zipper of the vest all the way to the top where you can only really see the knot with an inch or so of the tie, it's a really neat look. When tying a tie, the way to get a perfect knot at the end is by placing your thumb behind the front of the knot and dig in when you're sliding it up from the base. I'd stay away from ties with square bottoms (this isn't Milan or Paris fashion week). I also think cloth or cashmere ties look absurd. You see more bow ties than you think. I think they look incredibly goofy and should be avoided at all costs, but to each his own. For the last few years, colorful bold socks have been "in" on The Street, among traders and investment bankers, especially in Europe. I was never a huge fan of this style, and it already looks like it is starting to die out. However, I find on a casual Friday in the summer, it can really tie an outfit together. One thing in which I have seen an uptick that I don't

A Beginner's Guide to Success On The Street

personally like, but is becoming more socially acceptable, is wearing sneakers to work and then changing into shoes when you get there, or leaving them on all day. I get the reasoning, but I find it to be very low class. Sometimes in life, you must suffer practicality for class. *When in Rome...* There has always been a general rule in Finance, long before I started: When you're an analyst (first few years on The Street), don't dress like Gordon Gekko. Some people are stricter than others and come up with arbitrary rules that I personally think are dumb. For example, many say you should never own an orange Hermès tie until you're at least three years into the job. This is rubbish. For the most part, you can dress how you like. Wear bold ties, ties with clips, wear the occasional pocket square or shirt with designs. There are some things you really should refrain from if you don't want to look like a douche, or be called out by colleagues: a three piece suit, a shark skin suit, a watch you cannot afford on your salary (it was a gift from your parents), excessive jewelry, suspenders, suits that look like they cost more than $1K, a tie pin, an ascot. Avoid these styles until you're older, if at all, and you should be fine.

<u>Personal Styling</u>

Your hairstyle says a lot about you. When you were in high school and college, many people often styled their hair in crazy looks, e.g. Mohawk, etc. In high Finance, these hairstyles usually don't fly. The most common look on Wall Street is the Gordon Gekko or Patrick Bateman style: **slickback with gel. You can never ever go wrong with this look**. You'll know that you're slickback has become too long when it is parallel with the bottom of your earlobe in the back. You know it has become too thick when it requires multiple applications of gel to tap down closer to the scalp and slick back. Long hair for men is a no go, and for women past a certain point. Short hair on the sides, medium flip in the front is also another popular hairstyle for men. For women, it is usually harder to do a funkier hairstyle, but, if possible, I recommend staying away from bangs or very short hair.

For men, I always advise to avoid a beard. Many people grow beards these days in corporate America. But being from New York, working in New York, and rooting for the Yankees, I always have assumed the New York Yankees (George Steinbrenner) classic mantra: **No facial hair; we're classier than that**. Everyone is entitled to their own opinion, but I feel the clean-cut look presents you as a sharp well kept person. You don't generally see a lot of beards in Finance. November is really the only acceptable month to grow out a beard, as "no shave November" has become such a large cultural tradition these days. The same goes for other facial hair such as mustaches, Van Dyke, goatee, soul patch, etc.

<u>Eating Lunch at Work</u>

If you're a trader, you will be eating lunch at your desk, no doubt about it. For all others you should still probably eat at your desk. You will be able to eat and work at the same time, leading to increased productivity. If your bosses see you doing that, they will have a greater respect for you. Going out for an occasional lunch with colleagues is fine, but the usual routine is to go and grab take out and bring it back to your desk. The era of the "power lunch" has almost come to an end, with only Investment Bankers and those on the buy side still attending them on occasion. While the big lunches can help woo clients or keep them

A Beginner's Guide to Success On The Street

happy, you lose out on valuable time when you could be working. You know what they say: "time is money", and undoubtedly true.

The time you grab lunch is up to you. I personally like to get it later (1/1:30 PM) in the day so that by the time I'm done eating, it feels like the day is almost over. Others like to grab lunch earlier, then do a 3:30 coffee break, which is fine, too. Use this as an opportunity to get up and stretch a little, as sitting at your desk hunched over your computer all day will lead to "tech neck".

CHAPTER EIGHT: COMPLETING YOUR WORK

Whether you're doing work for your boss, someone on your team, or helping someone from another team / division, **always finish your assignment on time**. I can't emphasize this enough. Leaving work unfinished makes you look extremely bad. If you are close to finishing an assignment, stay late. Don't go home thinking that you'll "just come in early tomorrow". Unforeseen and unavoidable things happen all the time: you oversleep, the trains aren't running right, you get sick, etc. If for some reason you're not able to finish the work, either bring in someone to help you, or explain to the person that you intended to help that you simply don't have the bandwidth to finish right now, and that, while you're sorry, you're on top of it and will get it done as soon as possible. This also applies to new work. You always want to be proactive and ask for more assignments; but if you are asked if you are free to help on something, and you are not, it is OK to say that you cannot help right now because you are committed to completing an assignment for someone else. While your superiors may look at it somewhat negatively, they'll respect your honesty and levelheadedness. It's way better that you don't take the work than you half ass it and give it back to them either unfinished or poorly done (definitely a bad look!).

Never <u>ever</u> make BS excuses. Number one, they make you look bad. Everyone (including your boss) has his own problems and he's not interested in yours. *And if your excuse sounds phony, it probably is; you'll be found out, you'll look like an ass, and it's hard to recover from that.* It's basically a death sentence to be caught in a lie. No matter what,

From Main Street to Wall Street

don't lie to your boss. He'll find out and will never see you the same. No one (your boss especially) will ever trust you again.

<u>CYA</u>

You need to CYA at all times; that is, *Cover Your Ass*. If you're working on a group project and another individual isn't completing his/her portion, which will cause the whole thing to be delayed, you need to really motivate them, or get it across to your manager that you have completed your end of the project. A classic move is to be "too busy". You *do* want to take on more work if you have the bandwidth but *don't do it* if you will be drowned in work and the additional new assignments cause you to be unable to finish your current project and others (see above). You can also turn on the "busy" notification in *Outlook* often, which will discourage people from reaching out. You can turn on "do not disturb" in addition to "busy". This is really a preemptive CYA. The best way to CYA is with email. You can retroactively CYA by re-calling an email. If you are using Microsoft Outlook for email, there is a function called "Recall this Message" which will bring the message back to you if the intended recipient has not read the message already. You will have the option to either delete the message, or replace it with a new one. It's a very useful function whether the mistake is small or large; just be sure to recall the message ASAP. **In general, you don't want to put anything in writing that you don't want found out**. This particular scenario is the complete opposite. Documenting something in email, which will be time stamped, is the best way to defend yourself. If your boss says, "Hey, how come I never received this?", you can just forward the email you originally sent to him.

A Beginner's Guide to Success On The Street

Scapegoating the predecessor is also a CYA move, but has a limited shelf life. You can blame the person that came before you by saying the idea sucked, he/she couldn't run the project, and didn't explain the nuances of doing something clearly to you before leaving. However this only works for a short period of time, as you will be expected to learn things for yourself and do it better. If you continue to use this excuse after the first month or so, they will call you on your bullshit. It may have been someone else's bad idea/project when you first picked it up, but it eventually becomes yours and you don't want to have crap associated with your name; so either improve it, or ask your manager if it can be ditched. Don't be responsible for, or enable, someone else's failures; and don't get stuck holding the bag. In the end, you'll get blamed long after that other person is gone and forgotten.

If you need something done immediately, or you have requested something from someone but they have not responded, there are a few methods you can use to compel them to step up. The first is you can *cc* your manager. The higher up on the food chain he is, the better. By doing this you show your manager you're trying to get things done but are being held up by someone else. Your boss may either jump into the conversation or just respond directly to the delinquent party. Another option for you is to *cc their* manager on your request for performance and lack of same. By doing so, what you're really hoping to do is shame them into responding. Their manager then becomes aware that his employee has not been cooperative and that person usually moves quickly to help with your (t)ask. In an extreme situation, you can *cc* both their manager and yours. This should really be last resort as you don't want to make enemies, if you can avoid it. You never know whom you'll need later on. It's been said often that you should be nice to

From Main Street to Wall Street

people on your way up because you'll meet them again on your way down. It's all about maintaining positive relationships.

CHAPTER NINE: COMPANY SOCIALS

A disaster in the making and a potential minefield waiting for the innocent and naïve!

Company functions are a great way to connect with your colleagues or your boss on a more personal level. Whether it's an impromptu "let's grab drinks" with the team, a conference followed by dinner and drinks, or a company holiday party, you should **always ensure that you don't go overboard**. Depending on what area of Finance you're in will usually dictate how the get-togethers are orchestrated. While most of the Wolf of Wall Street or Boiler Room fanfare of the 80's is pretty much gone, some still like to work hard, play harder. In these precarious types of situations it's important to not be the one pushing the envelope, especially if you're the new guy/ junior guy on the team. For most people, you won't be entering that "rah-rah" era; but you will enter a situation such as a holiday party where you're at a nice venue with freely flowing drinks and unlimited food. Most people in Finance like to drink. That is a fact. However you don't want to become known as that person who got wasted at the company office party and acted like a jackass. A very bad look and a reputation that will haunt you for a long time. The point of these events is to let loose and have fun. So I think it's totally acceptable to get a nice buzz going, but that's about it. At the point where you begin to feel slightly tipsy and are slurring your words is the point that your next drink should be non-alcoholic, or downgrade from a mixed drink to a beer. It's really only OK to go all out when you're within five years age of your colleagues and your boss, and the more senior people on your team have already left the event. And even then...

From Main Street to Wall Street

This next piece of advice applies to company events, as well as in the office. **Try not to ever talk about politics**, and, if you have to, remain politically neutral. On Wall Street, there are generally two types of people: RR's and LL's. That is Rockefeller Republicans and Limousine Liberals. Of course there are always those farther to the right or left but for the most part a lot of people straddle the middle. Rockefeller Republicans are those who are staunchly pro tax cuts and de-regulation (of the Financial industry) and more socially liberal than conservatives, while Limousine Liberals are those that maintain a liberal outlook on social values but lean more conservative on economics, taxes, and de-regulation. If you are forced into a political conversation, unless you know the ideology of the other person, stay neutral, ask questions rather than voice strong opinions, appear interested and be a good listener. Silence is golden; diplomacy and tact trump all. No matter how much you know (or think you know), politics, like religion, is more emotional than intellectual. Zealots don't care about facts or reasoning. You will not change the opinion of someone across the aisle, and the more heated the conversation, the worse off you are, especially with someone senior in the company. Best to show your interest and knowledge by citing one of the more politically independent financial newspapers like the *Financial Times*, or *WSJ*.

<u>Office Relationships</u>

"Don't shit where you eat." This crude but common colloquial expression means do not have romantic relationships with any coworkers. Most such affairs, whether a casual fling or something more serious, have a bad ending. If you are in separate departments, it gives you a little more leeway, but I still strongly recommend against it, no matter what the temptation or your social situation. Office romances tend to blow up in your face. As I mentioned previously, happy hour or office parties have the potential to become a place where you embarrass yourself or make bad decisions. News and gossip travel fast. Any word of colleagues hooking up is prime water cooler gossip that steamrolls its way through the office, which can lead to others (including your boss and those in authority) seeing you in a negative light. Don't put yourself in that position. *Forewarned is forearmed.*

CHAPTER TEN: BE PROACTIVE

In life, it's rare that something ever just falls in your lap. The early bird gets the worm; grab the bull by the horns. There are a million quotes I could insert here but I think you get the point. If you want something, you have to go take it. If you keep your head down, do your work diligently, and show up on time you'll probably move up over the years. However you'll be invisible and no one will know you. Or you may be the guy who treads water for 20 years, runs in place, and is eventually let go to bring on an equally disposable new hire at a much lower salary. Getting your name out there in the firm is important for many reasons. If you're looking to make a lateral transfer at some point in the future, it's good to have people that will vouch for you that aren't only your immediate boss and team, i.e. from other divisions. Another good reason is that hopefully one day when you reach the point of becoming a Vice-President, an officer of the firm, you will need four firm officers (VP and up) to agree that you are fit to be such an officer and represent the company. This process is different for every firm. There are several things I recommend doing to get your name out there: become a mentor to a summer intern; join an upstart program or committee; actively aid in different charitable events; go meet with senior executives at the firm.

While it may seem unnecessary and even a time-waster, many executives are open to meeting with the younger people in the organization for two reasons:

1) They get to meet, interact, and know what kinds of people are joining the firm, the "new blood", and who their middle management is hiring; and

From Main Street to Wall Street

2) They get to see how their younger staff views the landscape, which can be very different than the direct reports they receive from senior management because of the age gap, skill set, and interest difference, and because senior management may say exactly what their directors want to hear instead of giving their true thoughts (more likely to come from the young, the inexperienced, the naïve, who still think honesty is the best policy—*imagine that!*).

CHAPTER ELEVEN: GENERAL TIPS FOR SUCCESS AT WORK

Tools

Yahoo Finance

Brightscope

EDGAR

Adobe Pro

Morningstar

Depending on your role you may be required to do surface level due-diligence on companies. *Brightscope* is a phenomenal resource for looking up the assets in both private and publicly traded companies' 401k Defined Contribution plans.

Searching for the cash on the balance sheet of publicly traded companies is easy as well. You can go to websites like *Yahoo Finance* or *Nasdaq*'s official website, type in the name or ticker of a company which should lead you to a list of statistics. By opening up the Financials tab, you can find the balance sheet where you'll be able to see the cash available either at the end of the prior year, or the most recent quarter.

Calculating the intrinsic value of company stock options and restricted stock units is also pretty straightforward. Go to the SEC's *EDGAR* Company's Filing website, and then type in the ticker or full name of the company. Locate the 10-K, and then search for the documents for the stock options, weighted average exercise price,

Restricted Stock Units (aka RSU, unvested or non-vested), and then go find out the current market price. To find the Intrinsic Value per option, subtract the weighted average exercise price from the current market price. To find the stock options' total intrinsic value, multiply the options outstanding by the intrinsic value per option. RSU total intrinsic value can be found by multiplying the number of RSUs by the current market price.

13D is a good form if you're looking to stalk hedge funds' positions, as it is required to be filed within 10 days of an investor acquiring a 5% or greater position in a publicly traded company.

13F is another good form to follow fund positions. It is required to be filed quarterly and shows the holdings of a fund regardless of the size of the position.

If you have the possibility of getting *Adobe Pro* at your firm, ask for it. The ability to convert files from PDF into Microsoft Word or PowerPoint is unbelievably useful.

On almost every PC that you use, Internet Explorer will be your default internet program. I regularly use IE as my go to browser but I find that it can be slow and clunky sometimes. Maybe I use it for nostalgia, or because it's most familiar to me. However, if you ever run into trouble with your internet browser freezing up or working too slowly, download and use Google Chrome. It is an extremely fast and efficient browser which will allow you to open many tabs at once, as well as interactive sites that require more processing power, and will not slow down your computer like Internet Explorer.

A Beginner's Guide to Success On The Street

<u>Meetings</u>

One thing I learned after a couple of months on the job is that every time you go into a meeting, whether it be with your boss or someone else, bring a pad and a pen, and scribble down notes. Unless you have a photographic memory, it's almost impossible to remember everything that was talked about or shown to you in a meeting. Taking notes helps you remember exactly what you need to do when you leave the meeting. Write the date / time if you can so you remember exactly when this happened and it will help give it context when you look back on it. Besides the obvious (that it will help you stay organized), the optics are very positive and it shows your boss that you are diligent, actively engaged, and following the conversation, and at least gives the appearance of being organized. [As an aside, I absolutely hate when people forget to cancel meetings they can't attend, or show up late to their own meetings (and this happens all the time…as a junior person, get used to it). If you have organized a meeting, whether it's in person, or over the phone, send out an email if you're going to be running late, or just cancel it altogether. Time is money, and it's annoying to have to wait there when you could be doing something else, because you're not sure if the meeting is happening or not. If it's your manager, or someone senior who organized the meeting, there's nothing really you can do other than sigh, or quietly fume to yourself. *To yourself* is the operative phrase. Keep your personal feelings *personal*.]

To take your organizational profile to the next level you should either have a running digital "to do" list on the home screen of your computer, or you can go old school with having a dry erase board on your desk, or whiteboard on your office/cubicle wall (very impressive if the boss drops in unexpectedly!). As you grow into your role, and become more senior, you will have an endless number of projects and due dates ranging from "immediate" to "months out" that are impossible to keep track of in your head. Having it clearly visible at all times and keeping it up to date will help you stay on top of things, which in turn will make you look like a superstar in front of your boss.

In addition to bringing all the necessary materials to meetings, come prepared to speak about something you've been working on related to the meeting, or a critique you can lob into the conversation. If your boss says, "Do you have any input or anything to add?" and you say "No", it shows that you're unprepared, haven't been following along in the meeting, or can't put forth the effort to think of something to add, even if it's small.

Always print out any meeting materials that were sent in advance and bring them with you. Your manager or the person running the meeting will look to see who brought it and is following along, and who is forced to take notes based on what some other person is saying. If the document is being presented on PowerPoint, bringing the presentation on a monitor notepad is fine; but if it is a handout, then you really should print it out. If you print out a few extra copies, you will get brownies if senior people forget to bring a copy and you have copies available for them. **Kissing up works!** Additionally it is ok to ask questions during a meeting, but don't be the individual who consistently interrupts to ask a question. Write down a list of all your questions, and go over it later (afterwards, privately) with the person hosting the meeting. Another thing you don't want to do is ask the same person too many questions; otherwise they may think you have a problem understanding the material or did not pay attention. If the questions are for your manager, try to limit them to the most important ones, and find someone else on the team you can have a separate conversation with subsequently to clear up any outstanding issues.

Corresponding with Your Superiors

For some reason it seems that the older you get at the firm, the more you write like a teenager using AIM (AOL Instant Messenger). Maybe it's because you become busier when you become an officer and you want to save time where you can. Regardless, when you're just starting out and speaking to people older than you, write in complete sentences, and try not to use acronyms. I frequently get IM'd or emailed asking "r u rdy?" or "I nd 2 go". If you're chatting with someone around your level, or someone you feel really comfortable with, that's fine; but really try to refrain. Responding in that kind of style, or using emojis, is seen as childish and unprofessional, and will most likely be looked down upon.

Smart Phones

If you have a work phone, bring it to your meetings so you can check urgent emails that may come in. **Do not bring your personal phone to a meeting.** It's incredibly rude to be texting during a meeting, especially if it's non-work related. **Unless you're a VP or higher, leave your personal phone at your desk.**

If you are given the choice between installing a work app on your phone to check email, or receiving a company phone, pick the latter. I firmly believe in a separation of church and state model. First, you *definitely* don't want to accidentally send something meant for friends and family to someone at work. This should help reduce the chances of that happening. Second, having a work email app on your personal phone will severely restrict what you can do, see, watch, download, and it will basically turn your life into a living hell.

Who needs that?

When I started, I received a Blackberry. I never liked Blackberries (I've always had an iPhone), but somehow I grew accustomed to having one. Maybe it was the keyboard, the simple functionality, or because it was synonymous with working on Wall Street. Around six months into the job, the firm said that everyone would have to surrender their Blackberries as we were switching to iPhones, which, surprisingly, left me a bit sad. However, I did enjoy knowing that I would be a part of the last generation to use Berries on The Street. Regardless, you have much more functionality with an iPhone and it makes it a lot easier to access documents.

Desk Top

Most companies give you the capability of working remotely by using a key fob with a random generating passkey or an app that does the same thing. In Finance, it is the norm to have a dual desktop setup at work. If you can afford it, it would be wise to try and replicate that set up at home, whether in your apartment or at your parents' house. That way, if you are sick, or are visiting family for an extended period of time, you can complete work just as efficiently as you would in the office. You're at your *virtual* desk in the office even though you may be elsewhere.

(Almost) Always Volunteer

If you are given the opportunity to work a rotation in another office, either domestically or internationally, you should *say yes immediately and unequivocally*, especially if it is an international assignment. While this has become rarer, especially with Brexit unfolding in our midst, it still occurs, especially in investment banking or ECM/DCM (Equity Capital Markets / Debt Capital Markets). Taking the leap will show your manager and the firm that you are a go-getter and not afraid to step out of your comfort zone to distinguish yourself and increase your skill set. You will also make invaluable connections along the way.

Connecting with your Manager

Building rapport with your manager is *essential* to advancing your career and enjoying your work in general. Get on his good side and your bonus could be significantly larger, and, even more important, he could be incentivized to help you get where you want to be, whether that is internally or externally. As an incoming analyst (or whatever a first year is called at your firm), you are unlikely to change managers often unless you are in a rotational program. Notwithstanding the foregoing, I experienced something I like to call "Manager Roulette". In my first year I had four different managers. One left the firm, and the other two moved into different roles. This left me having to start from square one with every manager. All the work I had put in previously, and credits I had built up, were now out the window. While frustrating, it is important to stay calm, cool, and collected, mush on, and be a good soldier (a "good corporate citizen" as one of my ex-managers put it). He said this when my team was relocated from downtown Manhattan near Wall Street all the way to Westchester, specifically Purchase, NY, which is right on the border with Connecticut. He knew that changing managers and now having to commute an hour and forty minutes was not ideal for me, but encouraged me to stick with it, as I was with a great firm, in a solid role, with a good new manager. Our separation was bittersweet as I moved on to my new manager; but, as I mentioned in a previous chapter, I always try to stay in touch with him from time to time because I never know when he may be able to help me, or vice versa. In my first year and a half, I went from starting in Westchester, then down to One New York Plaza, back up to Westchester, and then again back downtown. As it turned out, it was to be an ironic twist of fate: my new manager was going to be sitting in my old manager's office, and I would be sitting in my old seat. However this turn of events never actually came to pass. I ended up switching managers again, but at least this time had ample notice that I would be switching, as my current manager felt it best that I report to someone closer to my level and age so that I can grow as an employee and my manager can be more hands on with me. As a Managing Director, my previous manager barely had time to interact with me at all, and was busy making high level decisions instead of working on "nitty-gritty" assignments (the *raison d'etre* for new hires like myself).

In Finance, things change very rapidly. Teams move around, business units split up, and then get put back together years later. It's important to pay attention to what's going on around you, but sometimes there's really nothing you can do; just go with the flow and make the best of it.

A Beginner's Guide to Success On The Street

<u>Give Everyone Respect</u>

The janitor, the secretary, the assistant, the chefs in your building. Whether you're an incoming analyst, or a Managing Director, people around the office take notice, and nobody likes a jerk that belittles people below them. Good character goes a long way.

"A fisherman always sees another fisherman from afar" -- Gordon Gekko, *Wall Street.*

Money Never Sleeps. On Wall Street, real recognizes real. Seasoned veterans will recognize if you're a young shark in the making. If you're more reserved, don't pretend to be something you're not. It will only reflect badly on you. Personally, I've always thought of myself as a *Shark in a Sharkskin Suit* (patent pending; kidding; maybe not?).

<u>Naming Files</u>

So this is important for two reasons. The first is the most obvious: so you can track down files. Give the files specific names so you can find them when you need them, and begin creating folders for projects, people, or themes where you know you can continually go back there and find what you're looking for. Continually saving things in the general Documents folder will make it a lot harder to find old documents. The second reason is your manager may be a stickler, and/or the people you're sending the file to may not understand the premise of what's in it. Sometimes you'll have a file which you used for one thing and you will add or subtract information from it to use for something else, which then leads to a change in the theme of the file and becomes a new file unto itself. You should rename this file closer to the new theme

From Main Street to Wall Street

rather than keeping it the same name as before. **The devil's in the details!** It's little things like this that can help you stay organized and look neat.

As soon as you begin working on a new assignment, you should name and save the file. How many times have you worked on a project and all of a sudden the program freezes and crashes? You're frantically rebooting the program and hoping on the left hand side it says "Document Recovery" where it shows you the last version of what you were working on before it crashed (which may or may not be up to date!). By naming and saving the file in the beginning, you run a better chance that should your program crash, you have a relatively close version to what you were working on. If you really want to be secure, you can set up the "Autosave" feature that will save your work in intervals of however many minutes you like (FYI-- the default is 10 minutes).

Front/Middle/Back Office

When I was studying for my Series tests I used a tutor who gave me some advice that really stuck with me: **In life, there are Finders, Minders, and Grinders**. You have to decide who you want to be. *Finders* are essentially front office personnel; they are either client facing and bringing in the money and clients for the firm, or are a part of the research team coming up with great ideas. *Minders* are middle office people; they are the ones who are usually involved in business strategy for the firm and/or support operations that directly assist the front office. Lastly there are *grinders* who comprise mostly back office personnel; they are responsible for the gritty meticulous support, usually of

A Beginner's Guide to Success On The Street

functions that support the infrastructure of the business: Accounting, Human Resources, IT, etc. You have to decide what you are: a Finder, Minder, or Grinder?

<u>Work Hours</u>

Most people think that everyone on Wall Street works grueling hours; but trust me, there are plenty of "nine-to-fivers". If you are in a general Finance role you should aim to work at least from 7:30/8:00AM to 5:30/6:00 PM. Everyone has heard, "I'm the first one in the office and the last one out". People really do take notice if you're there when they're coming in, and still there doing work when they're leaving. It shows that you take your job very seriously; it's not just a paycheck, and in your superiors' eyes it shows that you are willing to put in the extra effort which will look good when it comes time for promotions. **The nature of the job will dictate your hours.** If you're on a trading desk, you'll be in the office extremely early going over investment ideas with colleagues and your manager. From there you'll sit at your desk practically without moving until the markets close. Almost immediately afterwards traders bolt and head for home. On a side note, if you are a sales trader, be prepared to entertain on a regular basis. You will have to take your buy-side clients out more than frequently to bars, dinners, sporting events or music concerts, which can be fun, especially when you're young, but you don't want to get burnt out. Many people burn the candle on both ends, which can have disastrous results.

Investment banking hours are longer, and are the reciprocal. Usually Investment Bankers work extremely late on presentations for clients so that they can close deals. In doing so, they are usually allowed to come in later. I have seen some bankers be allowed to walk into the office as late as 10 AM. If you have the luxury of coming in on the later side, you should consider being self-productive in your off-hours, such as going to the gym. Despite (or maybe because of?) the thrill and electricity of the markets on a second-to-second basis (an adrenaline/endorphin rush in and of itself), it's important to have some downtime, away-from-work (physically, mentally, and emotionally), to maintain your sanity. Personal time is not wasted time. Schedule time to see your friends, have a social life, **take care of yourself**, or else you'll get exhausted and sink. **Balance is key**. Remember: **a successful career in Finance is a marathon, not a sprint.**

Outside Business Interests

When you start working, you must disclose any outside business interests, or OBI's, that you might have. If your outside work activity is perceived in any way as a conflict of interest (i.e. involves something that could negatively influence your work decisions, or competes in the same industry as you and against your firm), it will almost always be prohibited, and you will be required to stop if you want to continue working there. Occasionally some OBI's are accepted, especially if what you're doing is relatively minor, or in a completely different field. Failure to disclose an OBI could lead to your prompt termination (and a red flag in your HR file for future reference), so it's important to be up front about it. One thing, especially in Finance, that you need to disclose is your financials. If you hold your assets at another financial firm, you need to disclose where they're being held. It is much easier to move your (and, if possible, your family's) assets to the firm (especially if it's a bulge bracket bank) that you'll be working at. This is what I did. So far, so good.

<u>SWOT</u>

A SWOT analysis (Strengths – Weaknesses – Opportunities – Threats), is something I learned from my mentor in middle school. It's a constructive way to evaluate why your product (or business, firm etc,) has a competitive advantage, the things that leave it vulnerable, opportunities to improve it, and finally issues that could cause trouble down the line. One can also use a SWOT analysis to critique himself. You may find it hard to criticize yourself objectively. However, if you can commit to filling out a chart with a few attributes for each section of the analysis, you will come away with some valuable information and insights about yourself, including where to improve. **This only works if you're honest with yourself.** If you're not, who are you kidding?

CHAPTER TWELVE: COMMUNICATION USING FIRM EQUIPMENT

Whenever you use a device connected to your firm's servers, assume that you are being watched by Big Brother. The Brave New World is here, and we are constantly being surveilled in all venues, especially at work. This includes texting from a company phone, emails, chat messages, and calls from your desk phone or company phone. The most closely watched messages are the email and chat messages. These media of communication are not monitored infrequently and usually look for key words that may spark a review. As noted earlier, **if you wouldn't want your boss to read it, you should probably not put it in writing** as a general rule. Opt for the phone, or better yet wait to speak in person. The less you use firm equipment to talk about personal matters or gossip, the less you put yourself in jeopardy.

When you start at a firm, they usually begin by saying, "Never use your work email to send messages outside of the firm." That's not exactly or entirely the case. You can generally use your email to send messages to people outside of the firm, or even to your personal email, as long as they do not contain any proprietary information. For example, if you bought tickets to a sporting event on your work computer and wanted to send them to your personal email address, that would be ok. This is usually the case, but double check with your company (HR) as every firm has its own policies regarding the issue. The one thing you *must never* do is send so-called classified business documents to your private account (*see Hillary Clinton*). If you don't have the ability to work remotely, then that is too bad. **I repeat: do not send information**

From Main Street to Wall Street

to your home account as you will most likely be flagged for review and then possibly be suspended, or fired. You will undoubtedly have some sort of punitive blowback. You need also be careful about sending confidential information *internally*. Your group may be privy to information that another group in the firm is not, and by sending it to someone who should not have access (or *cc*'ing it, or "reply all" to a party who should *not* be in the loop), you risk getting flagged where you would go to an internal review. You are likely to get a reprieve the first time if this was done by accident; *but you should not put yourself in that position in the first place.*

CHAPTER THIRTEEN: ALWAYS BE PREPARED

You never know when you're going to have to meet with someone very senior on an impromptu basis. This is why you should always keep a tie in one of your desk drawers. Ideally you'd keep a sports jacket in the office as well; but because you likely won't have an actual office, it will probably be hard unless there is a coat hanger you can attach to your cubicle / section.

Other things you should keep in your desk:

Deodorant, toothbrush, mouthwash, gum/mints, toothpaste, floss, comb, hair gel (or any derivative thereof), and cover up.

People have bad mornings, or long nights, where you may not have time in the morning to look your best because you were out doing "Models & Bottles" last night and now you're running late. Or you have an important meeting later in the day that you want to freshen up for. Or you are going out with colleagues for drinks or a company social later and you want to be fresh. Regardless of the reason you want the ability to be on your "A" game. Don't be caught flatfooted; be ready to step up at any time. That's what's expected of you and can make the difference between a promotion and a dismissal.

The View From The Bottom

Most people starting out in the industry are trying to keep their manager happy, and not get fired. By building up some tenure, and diversifying your skill set, you have prioritized building a moat around yourself. Things are relatively simple when you're an analyst or an associate: **Show up early, leave late, exceed expectations on work projects, and maintain a good relationship with your manager and team.** This will help you get promoted in your first few years on the job. But, as you move up in the firm, the game changes. It's not necessarily a simple meritocracy anymore, but, as my grandma used to say, it's more and more how you play the game. As I specified earlier, reaching out to others around the firm and building your connections is essential, and the earlier you do so, the better. Wall Street is hyper-competitive, and so many individuals are ruthless and cutthroat. This is why it's important to always CYA, and be on your guard. It gets harder to move up once you become an officer of the firm, which is why those that are hungry begin scheming early on for their best approach to the top. While not everyone operates like this, it is not infrequent, and you should watch out for those that may look to backstab you. **Your "friends" may or not be your friends. Never burn bridges.** People have memories like elephants and will hold grudges to their deathbed. That person you crossed, or that enemy you once made (from time immemorial) in your firm, might be the one halting your progress, or torpedoing your promotion later on.

However if you feel like you're about to be stabbed in the back, you should think to yourself, in the words of Anthony Scaramucci, "I'm a Wall Street guy, and I'm more of a front-stabbing person".

CHAPTER FOURTEEN: VACATION

When you start out, you don't usually get a lot of vacation time, although sometimes you are blessed (as I have been, fortunately). When you begin your career it is usually best that you don't take more than five business days in a single block. You want to show your boss that you are committed to your work and the company. To increase maximum efficiency, center your vacation around weekends and holidays so you can squeeze in an extra few days on both ends without being on company time and the company's dime. You'd be surprised (amazed even!) how carefully you are being watched and judged all the time. At the entry level, you think you're invisible and under the radar? Not to HR you're not! It is important to save a couple of vacation days for emergencies. While companies usually do have allocation for sick days, or your boss is ok with you working from home when sick, you never know when there may be an unexpected situation that requires you to be away from the office without access to a computer, basically off the clock. Bank some time for that eventuality.

When you do take formal vacation, you should really try to relax, and leave work behind. **However, if you have an important meeting that you would ordinarily miss by being away, dialing in from another country while on vacation will absolutely give you extra brownie points with your boss.** Not only will it impress him, but you'll actually be able to get a first hand account of what's going on, and contribute, as opposed to a second hand report (at a later date) of what happened. You want to remain in the mix and relevant, and definitely don't want your boss to realize that they can do without you! I have personally done that

From Main Street to Wall Street

many times, including from Italy, Hong Kong, London and Puerto Rico. Every time I have called in from vacation, my boss commended me, and then, at the conclusion of the call, would kiddingly tell me to go enjoy my vacation because he was going to put me to work when I returned. I like to bring my work phone with me and occasionally check my emails so I can tangentially stay in the loop, but also so that I do not have to be faced with hundreds of emails the following week when I get back. That is something I dreaded the first time I went on vacation and then returned back to my desk. While the ability to be off the grid is nice, being accessible to your manager 24/7 is something that he will profoundly respect and take notice of (even though it's a pain in the ass. Get used to it. That's life in Finance. If it's not for you, I suggest you find another field.).

Another important tip is to avoid extended vacations in the month of February. February is bonus season, so you don't want to take off right before your check comes in. It may leave a bad taste in your manager's mouth, and that's the last thing you want when he's the one deciding how much you will receive. I recommend either before February or any time after the last week of February, although going on vacation in the last few days of February going into March should be fine. Two other times I recommend holding off on vacation are around Thanksgiving and from Christmas to New Year's. At that time many senior people (who have paid their dues and earned it) are either working from home, or are on vacation. This will give you the opportunity to catch up on work while the office is quiet, catch up on studying for any tests/certifications you may be trying to take, or work from home yourself in a more relaxed environment. Since the office slows down around these times, especially late December, it will almost be like a free holiday, so there's no point in scheduling a week off of your hard earned vacation days. By not taking

A Beginner's Guide to Success On The Street

off, you also assure your boss or others that there is someone there to hold down the fort. So it's a double plus. You really should also try to stick around in late December / early January. This is when you usually have a 360 year-end review where the manager goes over what you did well, and what you can improve on (what you didn't do well). Shortly after that you will have Compensation Day, which is called something different at every firm. It is the day you find out what you're making next year, what your bonus is, if any, and if you're going to be promoted. It is a happy day for some, and a not so happy one for others. Every year-end review is different. Some managers are very brief; they go over your pros and cons and then basically kick you out of their office. It is just a required directive of the firm and they want to get back to work. Others take a more thoughtful and meaningful approach, having more of a discussion, allowing you to ask questions regarding how to improve, questions about the business, your future career paths, etc. It's rare that your manager will ask you to critique yourself, but you should be prepared to do so anyway. You don't want to throw yourself under the bus, but you also don't want to be too soft. Think of realistic criticism, and then tone it down one notch. If, for whatever reason, your manager asks you to criticize him, **absolutely do not do it**; complement him, whether you're really feeling it or not. Your public face and your private face are two entirely different things and never the twain shall meet. **Insulting your manager is professional suicide**.

CHAPTER FIFTEEN: COMPANY CREDIT CARD / WORKING LATE

This should go without saying, but if you are lucky enough to receive a company credit card, you need to be responsible with it. In the words of Uncle Ben from *Spiderman*, with great power comes great responsibility. Whether you're a sales trader taking out buy side clients, an investment banker wooing large banking contracts, or just someone who may need access to company funds for small things like ordering supplies, it is essential that you stay within the limits of your card. The process for filing reports on expenses, at least at bulge bracket sell side banks, is very tedious. Mistakes are not taken lightly, someone is watching every penny of expenses (that's his job!), and HR will track everything you buy on the card, line item by line item. While an occasional mistake is ok, finding glaring errors (that you were not entitled to) on your card will result in revoking of the card, suspension, or being flat out fired (and, needless to say, a demerit on your permanent record). Even those without a company card can usually expense things to the firm, but, again, it should be done sparingly, meticulously documented, and on an as needed basis only. Every bank / firm is different, but most will let you order dinner on the firm when you're working late at the office, and then call an Uber / taxi / limo home after a certain hour, usually after 7 or 8 pm. Again you should really only use this if you are staying late and working. *Membership has its privileges (as long as you don't abuse them).*

CHAPTER SIXTEEN: WHAT TO DO WHEN TIMES ARE ROUGH AND THINGS AREN'T GOING AS WELL AS YOU HOPED

My Personal Trials, Challenges, and Road Map to the Promised Land

When you're in high school, for the most part either your parents or a favorite teacher will be your mentor. They can help play a big part in shaping your future and you should turn to them for advice, especially your parents, as they have nothing but your best interests at heart, and will want to give you nothing but support to help you succeed. You will have many different supporters as you progress through different stages of your life; however it's important to find one that is in your corner and in your field so he/she can give you advice based on experience. In New York and on Wall Street we call it "finding your Rabbi." I was lucky. My "rabbi" happened to be my across-the-street neighbor. I grew up hanging out with his son, and our families became close, so I saw him often. He was a real mover and shaker, someone who often wined and dined clients (and that appealed to me greatly!). He wasn't facilitating Investment Banking deals, or trading large sums of money; but he was a successful person on Wall Street who represented what I wanted to be. Often flying around the country, he helped raise capital for the hedge funds he worked at over the years. As an oenophile, foodie, and gourmet all in one, I always thought that the nature of his job was great. Even more appealing is that for a guy with a big personality, he always felt humble regarding his position, and described his job as "carrying the books", i.e. carrying the investment prospectuses to clients and trying to explain why they should invest money in his hedge fund. He taught me the initial ins and outs of Wall Street, helped me get my foot in the door, and to this day I lean on him for career advice. I know that if I am looking to make a career pivot, he can, and will, be instrumental in helping me secure a position I want. Some mentors are more of just a business relationship, such as an old manager at work; but it's even better, such as in my case, where you have a very informal/personal relationship with them and can meet for drinks to catch up, schmooze about the family and the neighborhood, while networking and picking their brains at the same time. **Life is all about relationships**. That's what makes the world go round.

My second mentor I met through the head of the Investment Management workshop at my school. I had come to him seeking help in finding a job. He knew I was not a part of his workshop, but I demonstrated that, for an undergraduate senior who did not finish up in the business program, I had a respectable understanding (for a novice) of Finance and the markets, and was clearly passionate, committed, and career-oriented. He allowed me to follow him on *LinkedIn* and to try to solicit any one of his connections, saying that I was under his guidance and looking for his help. I emailed hundreds of his connections (and, by the end of my search process for a job, easily over a thousand). My percentage of return emails was not very good (if I remember correctly it was something like ten). Two to three offered to help, and one actually did. He was a portfolio manager at Blackrock who offered to take a phone call with me. After we spoke, he became sympathetic to my situation. His story was amazing and inspiring. He was originally from Ohio, and attended Medical School. Late into the process he decided that he did not want to become a doctor, and moved to New York with no

A Beginner's Guide to Success On The Street

connections. He toured New York City looking for a job for over six months before he found a small buy side shop that would take him. He understood my situation, what it was like to come from a non-business background and try to break your way into the industry. For months he would send me job openings which he thought I should apply to, and when I would apply to jobs at his firm he always tried to write an internal recommendation. While his actions never directly helped me get a job, his motivation, guidance, and support were encouraging and helped give me the confidence to keep looking for a job even when things seemed bleak and banks were laying people off at the time.

It took me nine long hard months after graduating from college to land a job. At the time options were bleak. The stock market was in a major correction, and banks were cutting staff, especially in their fixed income divisions, freezing new hiring, and re-assessing headcount. I had interned at Northrop Grumman the summer prior which helped bolster my already strong belief in the continued expansion and success of the Aerospace and Defense industry. Wanting to go into a Wall Street research job that trafficked in A&D seemed like the ideal position for me at the time, so I decided to begin calling all the heads of research for defense at the major bulge bracket banks. I started with Goldman Sachs, as their A&D analyst was considered the best on The Street. Surprisingly I was able to find his direct office line on the internet. I called two to three times that week and no one picked up. Every week going forward I planned on calling until someone answered the damn phone. The following week his secretary answered the phone and said he was too busy; try again next week. This went on for about a month, and once he realized I wasn't going to go away and stop calling, he had his secretary set up a phone appointment. We talked for half an hour about what I was looking to do, my prior investment research experience, and he asked me

From Main Street to Wall Street

to pitch him a few stocks. I pitched Orbital ATK, a stock I was bullish on at the time, and one that I pitched as an M&A candidate while working at Northrop Grumman (it would eventually be acquired two years later, at a much higher valuation, giving me some satisfaction). He thought my ideology on stock picking was solid for someone out of college with no true experience; but he then asked me about my financial modeling skills. He told me that he had helped an individual before in a similar boat as mine, but he knew financial modeling inside and out. I did not have those skills, and he told me, very nicely, that without those skills he would not be able to help me. But he encouraged me to acquire them to make myself more marketable. I thanked him for finally taking my call and for the advice.

I met an individual through my Mom who worked as a sales trader at Raymond James and tried to help me get a job there and elsewhere. He was very nice and offered advice as well as a continued effort in trying to secure me a job. We met a few times for drinks to catch up, but nothing ever came of it.

Again, another break came from a connection my Mom had who's a patient's husband's friend and worked as a senior trader at Jefferies. He was younger than the guy at Raymond James and was also a good guy: friendly, truly doing his best to try to help, and seemed like someone you want to hang with on the weekends, which is a good trait in a colleague. He had me come in for several interviews with other traders on the desk in which I think I did very well. The position was given to an internal candidate but he continued to shop me around for other positions in the firm, which I interviewed for but ultimately did not get. He was apologetic that he could not help me more and told me to continue to keep my head up and keep pushing forward, "something will break", an

A Beginner's Guide to Success On The Street

expression I heard too often, which at times would leave me somewhere in between angry and frustrated. At this point I was a little down on myself. I had been searching for months and nothing had stuck. After Jefferies I began aggressively applying online again. I don't remember whether it was weeks or months but after applying to several positions on *efinancialcareers.com*, Deutsche Bank contacted me about a position in securities lending. I was very interested in the position, and the person who was my point of contact through the process was a very nice woman. I had gone in for several interviews and she had asked me to stay optimistic, and that she wanted me to have the job. I had a lot in common with the interviewers throughout the process, and I finally sat down with one of the individuals who helped run the entire unit. It was my fourth time interviewing there. He and I had a good discussion, and at the end he said, "Hey I like you, you have my vote, kid." I was ecstatic but tried to contain my optimism. I thanked him and shook his hand. I then left the building hoping to receive a call by the next week with an offer. The call never came. I emailed and called my point of contact asking what had happened. "Sorry, we're still in the midst of a hiring freeze." She said that everyone liked me, and that they *did* want to hire me, but were actually not allowed to. At this point I was devastated. Months go by and I'm still looking for a job. I'm really down on myself at this point, semi-depressed and needed something to lift my spirits. One of my closest buddies, who had landed a job at Citigroup right out of college, was planning a short trip to London and Dublin for a few days. On the behest of my mother I said I was going. I really needed this. Almost immediately after I booked my flight I was contacted by Morgan Stanley (Graystone Consulting) about an investment analyst position. They wanted me to have a phone interview with the head of manager research. **The relentless lobbying of my MS connection for over the**

From Main Street to Wall Street

past year had finally paid off. I said I was excited to interview for the position and could interview that week. But the individual interviewing me was on vacation that week and wasn't available until the following week, the week I was planning on going away. Though excited at the opportunity, I was still upset at my prior experiences/disappointments, and decided not to cancel my trip. I really needed this vacation, especially if this job wasn't going to work out either. I thought to myself, "This is a phone interview; what does it matter whether I'm in New York, or London? Most likely he's going to want to do the interview in the early morning, which will be fine with me since it'll be in the afternoon in the UK. If he wants to do the interview later in the day, that's still fine; it won't be later than 10 PM in my time zone." So I scheduled the interview, 9:30EST/2:30GMT. I had walked around Harrods, a very posh designer store in London, the morning of my interview to do some window shopping. You really see some outrageous things there you won't find anywhere else in the world. Around 1:30 I left to grab a large pint before my interview. I wouldn't recommend drinking before an interview (or doing it while on vacation in another country for that matter), but I felt this was my last real shot at a job in Finance and I wanted something to take a load off, and settle the nerves a bit. After my beer I left and ended up on a quiet street somewhere that intersected all the major luxurious districts of London: Kensington, Knightsbridge, Chelsea, Belgravia. I thought it was a fitting place to conduct a phone interview for a job in Finance. I was worried I would have issues receiving the call; thankfully I didn't. A few minutes after 2:30 a call came in from a New York number. I answered. The phone interview went extremely well. Almost as soon as I hung up, I walked straight to the closest cigar shop and bought Cuban Cigars. I had a good feeling about Morgan Stanley and planned on celebrating. I was happy

A Beginner's Guide to Success On The Street

and optimistic for the rest of my trip. I went on many in-person interviews with MS once I returned state side, and became nervous that I would face yet another "Deutsche Bank" disappointment. But finally, after almost a year of interviewing, I was offered a job! After such a long, tedious, and stressful journey, what an unbelievable (incomparable) relief.

Thank you, Mom, for all the effort you put in continually pursuing every lead, and asking every person you knew if they could help me get a job. This beer's for you!

CHAPTER SEVENTEEN: PERSONAL GROWTH

Investing / Retirement Savings

Almost all companies in Finance, and America today, offer a 401K match program. This is where they will match whatever percentage of your salary you decide to invest into the 401K, up to a certain percentage (usually somewhere between 3-6%). Ideally you'd like to put up the maximum percentage because the matching funds are essentially "free money". If you are living at home with your parents and commuting to work, I highly recommend "maxing out" your 401K. Unfortunately this is not always possible, especially if you are living in New York, as apartments and living expenses are high; but you should be investing in your 401K, even if it's only 1%. *It's free money!! And get started early!* **As Albert Einstein once said, the power of compound interest is the most powerful force in the universe**.

In addition to your 401K you should set up a Roth IRA. An IRA is another type of retirement savings account; the Roth prefix makes it so that you pay tax on the money you are investing, as opposed to when you finally withdraw your money in retirement (regular). Both earnings on the account and withdrawals after age 59 ½ are tax free. A Roth IRA has the following stipulations: you can't make over $125K a year, and you can't invest more than $5.5K a year. Until you reach the salary cap you should try to invest the maximum into this vehicle as well. It will only help expand your personal wealth for retirement.

Finally there are "Rollover IRAs". Sometimes, if you had a long summer internship at a big company, they are obligated to start a 401K or IRA for you. You can roll it over to wherever your financial advisor is located and continue to build on that. Even if it is very small (under $100), you should go through the process of rolling it over to have another retirement vehicle to invest in. Investing early will not only help accumulate wealth for retirement, but is important in case of a market or economic downturn if/when Wall Street starts cutting jobs.

As a side bar, if you are ever offered a golden parachute, take it and run. Dragging it out with HR and/or trying to negotiate it usually results in a lower exit package. Be the first guy out the door, not the last. That way you will have something to stand on, and be the first guy in line looking for a new job.

The Ten Commandments

I. ABOVE ALL, BE TRUE TO YOURSELF; CHOOSE YOUR OWN PATH

II. KEEP YOUR HEAD ON A SWIVEL; ADJUST TO CHANGING REALITIES

III. WHEN TIMES ARE ROUGH, SOLDIER ON AND POWER THROUGH

IV. IT'S NOT WHAT YOU KNOW, BUT WHO YOU KNOW—NETWORK, NETWORK, NETWORK

V. PERSISTENCE PAYS OFF

VI. KISSING UP WORKS

VII. NEVER STOP LEARNING

VIII. WORRY ABOUT EVERYTHING, BUT DON'T LET IT PARALYZE YOU

IX. SKATE TO WHERE THE PUCK IS GOING, NOT WHERE IT HAS BEEN (Wayne Gretzky)

X. IT'S FINE TO CELEBRATE SUCCESS, BUT IT'S MORE IMPORTANT TO HEED THE LESSONS OF FAILURE (Bill Gates)

Epilogue

I can truly say that my first year and a half on Wall Street was a success. I managed to get two certifications under my belt, was promoted, salary raised, and given a larger than expected bonus. I have networked around the firm from as low as other analysts (like me) all the way up to an eminent Vice Chairwoman who was willing to take time out of her extremely busy schedule to meet with me on several occasions. I switched locations four times, have had four different managers and it looks like I will have another manager this year. *I don't know exactly where I'll end up or what I'll end up doing, but I do know I want one thing: **more!!***

Glossary

Wall Street Jargon-Vocabulary

There are a lot of terms you will hear when you begin working on Wall Street that may be unfamiliar. For any you may encounter that are not on this list, visit *Investopedia.*

This is a starter pack to help you get going:

Alpha- Return on an investment against the market

All Or None (AON)- An order to buy or sell securities in their entirety; it does not need to be immediate but must be done by the end of the day or canceled

AUA- Assets Under Administration/Advisement

AUM - Assets Under Management

Bearish- Pessimistic outlook

Beta- a measure of volatility that demonstrates whether a security is more or less volatile than the market as a whole

Big Swinging Dick- This is the rainmaker at the firm bringing in the most clients and largest deal; a boss

Boiler Room- Shady firms selling penny stocks or selling equity in fake companies

Boutique Investment Bank- Smaller more specialized investment banks *that don't offer all the services that bulge brackets do

Building a book- Increasing your client base

Bulge Bracket- The largest multinational investment banks

Bullish- Optimistic outlook

Bulls, Bears, Pigs- *Bulls* make money (longs), *Bears* make money (shorts), *Pigs* get slaughtered (those who are greedy)

Buyback- When a company repurchases its stock

Buying Size- Trading a large amount of money, or a large amount of securities

Carried Interest- a proportion of the profits partners market at Private Equity firms in excess of the Hurdle Rate

Cash(ed) Out- When someone successful decides to leave after a successful career, or sell securities based on a big financial gain

Chicago Board Options Exchange (CBOE) Volatility Index- shows the market's expectation of 30-day volatility

Clowngrade- When a sellside analyst upgrades or downgrades a stock for a stupid reason

Dark Pools- Private exchanges where institutional buyers and sellers can trade securities and liquidity while disguising or not making their orders shown to the public

Dead cat bounce- a temporary recovery from a prolonged move downward

A Beginner's Guide to Success On The Street

Dog with Fleas- An underperforming stock or security with a lot of problems

Downside- potential risk

DRIP - Dividend ReInvestment Plan

Dry Powder- Cash you keep on the sidelines to use to purchase securities at a favorable price, i.e. when there is a dip, M&A transactions, or short term debt

Fallen Angel- A bond that was given investment grade but has since fallen to junk

Falling Knife- A stock or security that has fallen in value rapidly. Don't try and catch it; you'll lose your fingers (lose a lot of money)

Fat Finger- A computer error where a person pushes the wrong button, or enters in the incorrect amount and causes a much (usually) larger or smaller trade to occur

Fill Or Kill- *An* order to buy or sell a stock in its entirety, immediately, or not at all

Fear Index (VIX)- Synonymous with the VIX, it is the ticker symbol for the Chicago Board Options Exchange (CBOE) Volatility Index

Free Cash Flow (FCF) – Cash Flow - CapEx

Fuck You Money- enough money where you could retire and live life however you want to

Fuck You Pay Me (FUPM)- Used especially in Investment Banking: when you feel you are doing most of the grunt work and are being underpaid, you demand that you receive a higher compensation and bonus

Give me some color on that- Provide some additional details on that to make things more clear

Good Till Canceled (GTC) Order- An order to sell or buy a security at a specific price that stays active until executed

Hardbody- Attractive Woman

Hardstop- You have to end the meeting exactly at the scheduled time because you have another meeting directly after

Hedgistan- The area located between Manhattan and Westport, CT on the I-95 corridor, encompassing Greenwich, CT, the "hedge fund capital of the world"

Hedgefund Hotel- When a stock's main investors are hedge funds which are usually there for a short period of time. When all the hedge funds leave at the same time the stock will collapse

Herd Behavior- When many people pile into the same trade, either join in and ride the wave or bet against it and be contrarian

High Finance- Talking about those who do the big deals on Wall Street; also used sarcastically to talk about working in Finance in general

High Frequency Trading (HFT)- Trading using powerful computers that use a variety of complicated algorithms to conduct trades at extremely fast speeds

Hunting Elephants- Looking for big deals; made famous by Warren Buffett

Hurdle Rate- Minimum rate of return required

Junked Up- Super Bullish

A Beginner's Guide to Success On The Street

Immediate Or Canceled (IOC)- Buy or sell whatever portion of securities you can immediately, and cancel the rest of the order

Levering Up- In portfolio management it is when you take on debt to potentially multiply your investment returns, or in Corporate Finance it is taking on debt to fund a new project or for M&A

Limousine Liberal- Hypocritical wealthy left wing liberals: 10 degrees to the left of center in good times; 10 degrees to the right of center if it affects them personally (see Phil Ochs: *Love Me, I'm a Liberal)*

Long- betting for something to succeed/go up

LRC - Legal Risk Compliance

Middle Market – Investment bank that provides the same range of services as bulge brackets but on a smaller scale

Net Income - Profit

Odd Lot- Less than the normal unit of trading for the security, usually less than a hundred

OOO - Out Of Office

Perma-Bear- Someone who is always bearish on the markets

Perma-Bull- Someone who is always bullish on the markets

Piker- Someone who thinks and pretends to know everything about Wall Street, but in reality knows nothing

Painting the tape- Buying and selling a security to create the appearance of high volume to drive the price up

Quant- Quantitative Analyst

From Main Street to Wall Street

Rat Hole- An individual who owns securities (a front man) on behalf of another individual secretly, or a place where you secretly stash cash

Rockefeller Republican- moderate or liberal Republican

Shop- firm

Short- betting for something to not succeed/go down

Short Squeeze- When a heavily shorted security moves higher forcing short sellers to close out their positions and adding to the upward pressure of the stock

Sold!- A sarcastic way of saying definitely not

Stick- 1 Million dollars; or a cigar

Tax Inversion- When a company moves its HQ to a lower tax domicile / tax haven to reduce their corporate taxes by physically moving the Headquarters or by having an international company buy their operations and then having the new entity assume the headquarters

The trend is your friend- Usually an extended move in a security up or down will continue; don't try to fight it

Upside- potential gains

UHNW- Ultra-High Net Worth

What is your bandwidth?- Do you have any additional free time to work on a project for me?

Whale- Very large prospect/client

What is your schedule like this weekend?- I want you to clear your schedule to do some more work

A Beginner's Guide to Success On The Street

WFH - Work From Home

Whiteshoe Firm – One of the top firms in banking, law, or consulting

CPSIA information can be obtained
at www.ICGtesting.com
Printed in the USA
BVHW09s0933030918
526376BV00020B/731/P